CW01466535

DISCLAIMER

The contents of this book are for information only and are intended to assist readers in identifying symptoms and conditions they may be experiencing. This book is not intended to be a substitute for obtaining proper medical advice and must not be relied upon in this way. Always consult a qualified doctor or health practitioner. The author and publisher do not accept responsibility for illness arising out of the failure to seek medical advice from a doctor. In the event that you use any of the information in this book for yourself or your family or friends, the author and the publisher assume no responsibility for your actions.

The author and publisher have made every effort to ensure that the information in this book is correct at the time of printing and do not assume, and hereby disclaim, any liability to any party for any loss, damage, offence or disruption caused by errors or omissions, whether such errors or omissions result from negligence, accident, or any other cause.

Copyright © Dr Libby Weaver, 2019

Published by Little Green Frog Publishing Ltd

Publication design and illustrations: Stephanie Don. St. Clement Creative www.stclementcreative.com

Photography: Sabine Bannard www.sabinebannard.com

www.littlegreenfrogpublishing.com

ISBN: 978-0-473-48184-1

Printed in China

The INVISIBLE LOAD

A GUIDE TO OVERCOMING
STRESS & OVERWHELM

DR LIBBY WEAVER

RUSHING WOMAN'S SYNDROME — DR LIBBY WEAVER

Accidentally OVERWEIGHT — Dr Libby Weaver

EXHAUSTED *to* ENERGIZED — DR LIBBY WEAVER

BEAUTY FROM THE INSIDE OUT — DR LIBBY WEAVER

Dr Libby's **The Calorie Fallacy** — DR LIBBY WEAVER

THE BEAUTY GUIDE | DR LIBBY WEAVER

Women's Wellness Wisdom | DR LIBBY WEAVER

WHAT AM I SUPPOSED TO EAT? | DR LIBBY WEAVER

The ENERGY GUIDE DR LIBBY WEAVER

REAL FOOD KITCHEN | Dr Libby Weaver

Dr Libby's Sweet Food Story — Dr Libby Weaver with Chef Cynthia Louise

Dr Libby's Real Food Chef — Dr Libby Weaver with Chef Cynthia Louise

ALSO BY DR LIBBY WEAVER

For Maddy,
with star-filled
thanks

Contents

Overwhelm verb

over·whelm | \ ˌō-vər-ˈhwelm, -ˈwelm\
overwhelmed; overwhelming; overwhelms

Definition of *overwhelm*
transitive verb

1: UPSET, OVERTHROW
The tornado *overwhelmed* many mobile homes.

2a: to cover over completely: SUBMERGE
The city was *overwhelmed* by the flooding caused by the hurricane.

b: to overcome by superior force or numbers
The city was *overwhelmed* by the invading army.

c: to overpower in thought or feeling

overwhelmed with grief
overwhelmed by terror

A sense of inadequacy *overwhelmed* me.
overwhelmed with guilt

Synonyms for *overwhelm*
crush, devastate, floor, grind (down), oppress, overcome,
overmaster, overpower, prostrate, snow under, swamp, whelm

An additional note from the author:
While the word 'overwhelm' is technically a verb, it is used throughout this book,
at times, as a noun. Somehow this fits best with the sense of being overloaded,
engulfed by hectic daily activities and stress.

Load noun

/ləʊd/

Definition of *load*

transitive verb

1a: the quantity that can be CARRIED at one time by a specified means especially a measured quantity of a commodity fixed for each type of *carrier*—often used in combination: a boat*load* of tourists

b: whatever is put on a person or pack animal to be carried: Pack—donkeys with heavy *loads*

c: whatever is put in a ship or vehicle or airplane for conveyance: CARGO—The ship was carrying a *load* of automobiles, especially: a *quantity* of material assembled or packed as a shipping unit

2a: a mass or weight supported by something: branches bent low by their *load* of fruit

b: the forces to which a structure is subjected due to superposed weight or to wind pressure on the vertical surfaces broadly: the forces to which a given object is subjected. Losing weight will lessen the *load* on your knees

3a: something that weighs down the mind or spirits: took a *load* off her mind

b: a burdensome or laborious responsibility: always carried his share of the *load*

4: a large quantity: Lot—usually used in plural. The boy had *loads* of toys

5a (1): the amount of work that a person carries or is expected to carry: his heavy *load* of day-to-day work

(2): the amount of authorised work to be performed by a machine, a group, a department, or a factory. The washer can take a 10-pound *load*

b: the demand on the operating resources of a system (such as a telephone exchange or a refrigerating apparatus)

6: the amount of a deleterious microorganism, parasite, growth, or substance present in a human or animal body—measure viral *load* in the blood; the worm *load* in rats — called also *burden*

7: genetic *load*.

Introduction

With a title like *The Invisible Load*, you'd be forgiven for thinking this is a book about how to reduce the things in your life that are causing you stress (and that probably feels pretty impossible right now anyway). While we could attempt this throughout these pages, once you removed the things from your list, it's likely, over time, you would fill it back up with other tasks and items—and that's because we won't have touched the heart of what's really driving your stress.

So, this book is different. This is a book about getting to the core of your stress and unravelling it once and for all.

Before I begin to talk about your invisible load and how to obtain visibility of the factors driving your stress, I want to illustrate just how intricately our thoughts and our biochemistry are interwoven.

Imagine we are on a bushwalk together at the height of summer in Australia. You're ahead of me, looking up at the trees as you walk, when all of a sudden I shout 'Stop! Don't move.' For a split second, you wonder what's happening and before I can warn you further, you look down and see the cause for my alarm (and no doubt now yours!)—there's a brown snake (the second most venomous land snake in the world) in front of you on the track.

For many of you reading this, you will likely have mentally conjured an image of a snake and the very thought of it has sent adrenaline surging through your blood, with its consequences, such as an elevated heart rate and a nervous feeling, now evident. Yet nothing has actually happened. You weren't literally in danger; you simply read some words. Your thoughts about this situation led your body to react in this way, driving a host of biochemical reactions. We do this every day while we sit at our desks and react to our emails or race through our day feeling pressured to get as much done as possible, and over time this can have a profound effect on our health.

When I work with people, I start by asking them questions about their health and then I move to asking how they feel in certain situations or about their body or life in general. I have heard powerfully inspiring stories and some that are too traumatic or heartbreaking to put into words. Some people get close to losing hope that life can ever be any better, while others remain optimistic, despite the most trying of circumstances. What I'm really doing when I question people is I'm listening for the sentiments between their answers for a glimpse into their invisible load. Understanding what our brain, and biochemistry, do with our experiences can truly change how we experience life.

Your invisible load is the weight you carry that silently drives the stress you feel, and because of its invisibility many people aren't even aware it's there. Yet we each can carry both a physical and emotional invisible load. It's what's in this load that actually prevents us from ever really getting to the heart of our stress.

Your physical invisible load is your body's reaction to stress, only it doesn't always look like this because often the stress response has been silently kicking off for years. It might show up one day in a tight neck and shoulders or body fat that seems to have crept on, both seemingly having come out of nowhere, yet both physical manifestations of the stress we carry. The invisible load on your body is often displayed in symptoms that seem frustrating—mostly because we don't understand why we have them. It's likely your body's invisible load is in action when you suffer with symptoms such as exhaustion, weight gain, uncomfortable periods or menopausal transitions, frequent headaches, or some thyroid troubles.

The invisible load on your emotions is constructed from your life experiences and the beliefs you have created from these experiences. And this filters across every thought you have.

You can imagine your invisible load like a pack full of rocks strapped to your back. Some rocks are old; you might have carried them for years or even decades, while other rocks might be new and were only added last week after a difficult conversation with someone you care about.

PERHAPS YOU FEEL AS THOUGH YOUR LIFE IS SO FULL THERE IS NOT ENOUGH TIME TO GET EVERYTHING DONE.

Is your overwhelmed schedule
leading you to live your life with an
underwhelmed Soul? And do you
long to change this?

DR LIBBY

The rocks aren't the 'things' that have happened to you; they're not the hard conversations you've had, the disappointments, or the number of items on your to-do list. The rocks are the thoughts, beliefs and meanings you've formed as a result of your experiences. You have unknowingly packed your own backpack and it's weighing you down physically and emotionally.

Inside your pack there are rocks with beliefs about who you have to be to feel loved—for example, successful, funny, kind, perfect, or a good person. There are some rocks dedicated to how you believe your life is supposed to look and others with beliefs about who you perceive you are as a person and how you want other people to see you. None of these rocks are inherently bad or wrong, but they do add a filter to your thoughts and impact on your biochemistry, your health and the stress you feel.

Have you ever noticed that sometimes you can walk past a pile of dishes on the kitchen bench and think, 'I'll get to that when I have time', while, at other times, you walk past a similar pile of dishes and decide that your whole house and life is falling down? Of course I'm exaggerating, but I'm sure the feeling is familiar.

If your invisible load is manageable then the dishes might only mildly bother you or you'll simply get on with tending to them. But if you're already feeling weighed down then the sight of the dishes might cascade your thoughts into complete overwhelm and that's when you decide your whole life is falling apart.

We think that we're stressed and overwhelmed by all the things we have to do in a day, and I'm not denying that for many of us our lives and responsibilities are often overflowing. But these aren't the cause of our stress. Your obligations and responsibilities are not your stress; it's your thoughts about those things in relation to yourself that cause it. And that's what I'm really hoping to help you understand in the pages that follow.

Please know that when I talk about stress in this book, I'm not referring to trauma but rather what people share with me are their everyday, moment-to-moment stresses. When I asked women in their twenties what stresses them out, the two most common answers I received were their Instagram profile, and their body—on page 174, you'll find out what this is really about and where this same stress could be showing up for you.

IT'S TIME FOR A NEW CONVERSATION ABOUT STRESS, FEELING OVERWHELMED AND HOW WE APPROACH OUR LIVES IN THE CURRENT CLIMATE WE FIND OURSELVES IN.

The things in our lives that we think cause our stress are easier to see—the confrontational colleague, the interfering mother, the never-ending barrage of emails and all of the tasks we need to do to keep a household running, juggling a million things and having to remember a million more.

Perhaps you're managing the needs of your family while trying to pay the bills, keep the house clean and the children nourished. Then there is trying to keep your partner, boss, friends, mother, father, children, colleagues, neighbours and even your friend's dog all happy, healthy and feeling appreciated, which feels like a full-time job in itself.

And, of course, you'd like to keep yourself fit and healthy—but given the task load you carry, much of which might also be invisible to others, it never feels like there's enough time for you. Throw on top of that concerns that unfold out of the blue, such as your health needing attention or the health of a loved one, comforting a distraught child, or the end of a relationship that you treasured and it's no wonder many of us are constantly feeling overwhelmed.

But don't get me wrong, many of these things you might love; it just feels like you never have enough time to enjoy them. But there are also the things that feel far from fun. Perhaps deep down you may even resent them. And with the weight of this responsibility can come a perceived lack of freedom, which can feel permanent and pervasive—two qualities that lead stress to have dire consequences on our physical, mental and emotional health when it goes on for too long.

Maybe sometimes you catch yourself wondering if this is all there is, if this is really what you signed up for. Surely there's more to life than meeting deadlines, folding laundry, replying to all the messages you receive each day, planning meals, getting the car serviced, grocery shopping, and working your tail off to keep the mortgage payments under control? Well, of course there is, but when you're feeling overwhelmed by the weight of your invisible load you may at times find it challenging to remember the beauty. You might also find it hard to recall what were once your aspirations and you've given up hope of ever realising them with the way you feel your life has to be now.

If we're really honest, it's more comfortable to believe that 'things, people and tasks' are the cause of our overwhelm—rather than our own thoughts. It's uncomfortable to accept that we might be causing ourselves so much suffering. But when we open to the possibility that we might actually be at the root of our stress response we can truly begin to overcome our overwhelm once and for all.

We can't control what happens in our day, but with awareness and practice, we can begin to catch a glimpse of how we're thinking. This is the ribbon we need to grab hold of in order to unravel our stress once and for all. It's catching these thoughts and beliefs that will ultimately alter our biochemistry, transform our health and our experience of stress, as well as how we live.

IT'S MORE COMFORTABLE TO BELIEVE THAT 'THINGS, PEOPLE AND TASKS' ARE THE CAUSE OF OUR OVERWHELM.

This book isn't necessarily here to tell you to slow down, to make a cup of tea and put a positive Pollyanna spin on the challenging situations you're facing. Although the human body does, of course, tend to benefit from downtime, leisure time and decent rest, as well as living at a pace and rhythm that is congruent with our nature. This book is not even about what you do. That's entirely up to you, of course. It is focused on how you think and how you undertake and perceive what you choose for yourself each day.

You can have a full and busy life that is not jam-packed with stress or sending you towards burnout or more serious health complaints. And in the pages that follow I'm going to help you to uncover how you might begin to create this for yourself.

Stress hormones, when produced constantly and relentlessly, have their own subtle and cataclysmic consequences. They also alter the function of many organs and body systems which contribute to your physical invisible load. We need to explore what is really driving stress—whether that shows up as a feeling of overwhelm, worry, anxiety or physical tension in the body—so our enjoyment of life, our relationships, as well as our health parameters (particularly our energy as that allows us to contribute) all improve.

Spotting your own invisible load takes immense compassion and kindness towards yourself, and I ask you to keep this in mind as you turn these pages. It involves turning the spotlight on yourself and it takes great courage to do this. In this book I'm going to take you on a journey to help you unpack your backpack and reduce the stress of your invisible load once and for all. We'll start by examining the impact of stress, worry and constant anxious feelings on your body. Then we'll explore how we think and the way we perceive ourselves and the world, and by the end of the book you'll be equipped with tools and insights to help you reduce your invisible load and overcome your stress and overwhelm once and for all.

It is possible to live a full life, brimming with possibilities, without the weight of your stress or that nagging feeling that there must be more to life. So, with all of this in mind, let's examine what stress really is for you and where it stems from. Let's look at your invisible load and also how you think about that load, your life, the planet and yourself.

Remember that life offers us innumerable opportunities for growth and learning in so many ways. And one of them is to trust. To trust the unfolding of it all because when we can trust, there's no reason to stress.

YOUR
LOAD

In order to address your invisible load, you first have to become aware of what it is comprised of. So with the kindness and gentleness with which you would approach a distressed child, let's begin to explore what your load looks and feels like. We will examine some common scenarios that can add to a person's invisible load and the consequential effect this has on their biochemistry. Always remember that true and lasting change comes from bringing only curiosity and leaving your judgement at the door— be tender with yourself.

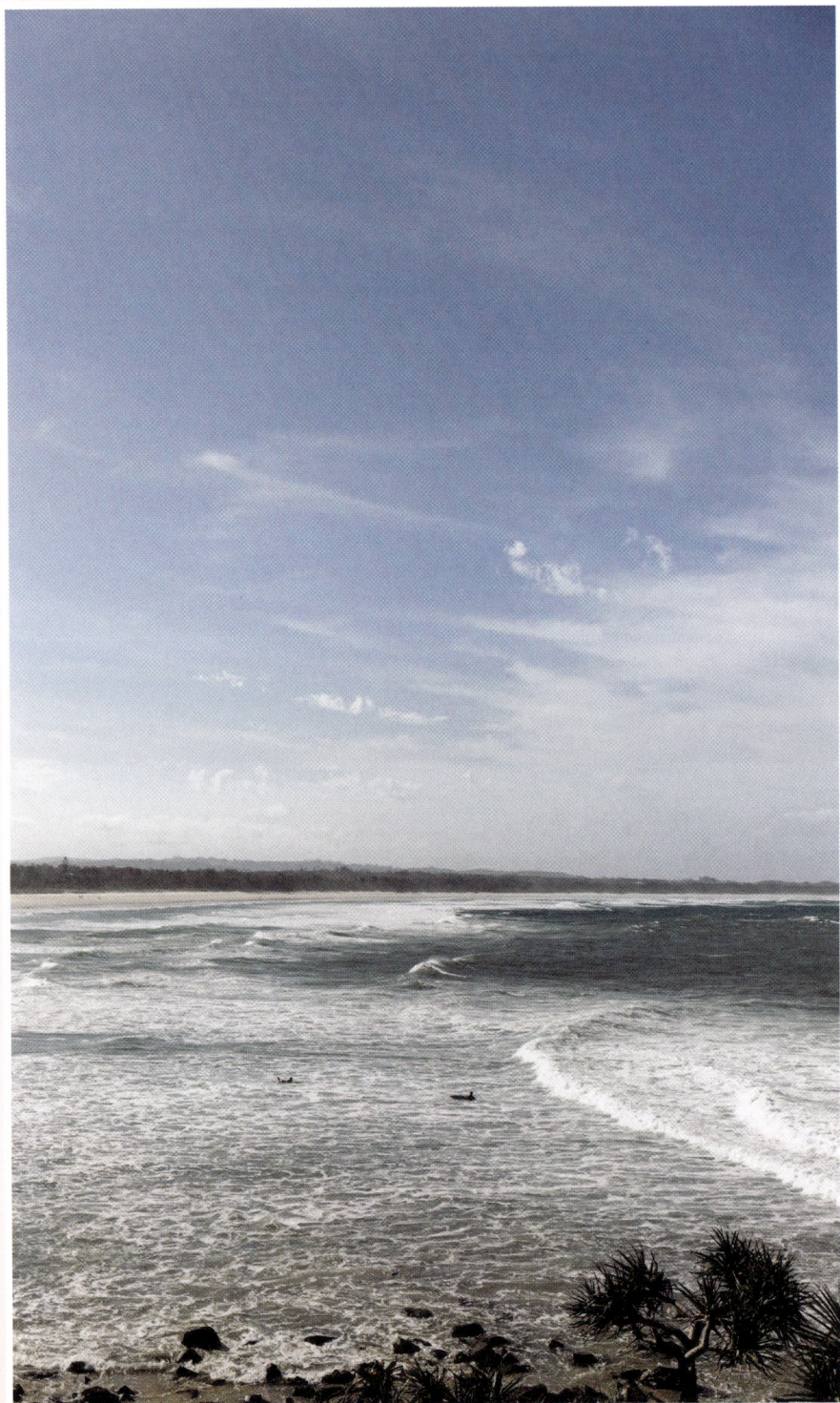

A familiar pattern of overwhelm

An example of the load

On a day-to-day basis, there are challenges in our lives that others may not realise you cope with. Some people share their problems openly, while others put on a brave face and may never let you see their struggles. It can be hard at times to even let yourself feel the anguish of a situation. Maybe you're adept at flipping your thinking away from what's on your plate to considering those less fortunate than you. And there is a beauty and grace and gratitude to be experienced in those thought diversions, but it doesn't take away from what you face each day: the things that your body or your brain—or both—might find difficult or confronting or just utterly exhausting and overwhelming.

As you will have read in the introduction, your invisible load is predominantly made up of the thoughts you think and beliefs you hold, but there's another factor that can unknowingly contribute to the weight of this invisible load and that's the choices you make on a day-to-day basis. You'll notice I used the word 'choice', and while when you feel overwhelmed it can seem like your choices are limited, each tiny choice you make can have a real impact on whether this adds to the burden of your invisible load or not.

Consider the flow-on effect of these choices below: many of them may feel familiar. We'll continue to unpack some of these throughout this book so if any resonate with you, note them down so you can explore them further.

HOW YOU CHOOSE TO FUEL YOUR BODY

When you feel overwhelmed most of the time, it's likely that as you go about your day the moments you have to yourself are fleeting and, more often than you'd like, convenience drives your food choices. This way of eating—relying too much on processed and takeaway food—means your nutritional intake is, at times, lousy. This quietly adds to your invisible load by affecting your ability to feel calm and energised.

Your Earth Suit (your body) has a basic biological requirement for nutrients that must be met. When that need is not met, internal stress occurs. For example, inadequate vitamin C or magnesium consumption can disrupt necessary cortisol production, which, regardless of what's going on in your outside world, leads to internal stress in the body from inflammation and fatigue. More often than not, convenience food does not contain enough antioxidants and this leads to oxidative stress on cells and tissues. So just through what you eat (or don't eat) alone, you're already contributing to your invisible load and putting yourself in a position that can lead to your body feeling overwhelmed.

CAFFEINE

When the days are busy and full it can feel as though caffeine (either coffee or energy drinks) is the only thing propping up your energy. Yet, caffeine increases your adrenaline and constantly elevated levels of adrenaline lead to everything feeling urgent. This means, if something unexpected occurs, you are more likely to overreact or change your perception of your day from 'manageable' to 'overwhelming' when the unexpected occurrence might not actually warrant that. Additionally, the alertness only lasts for a short burst, after which you crash, so you grab more caffeine or highly processed sweet 'food' to bring your energy back up again. Behind the scenes, biochemically, the effect of caffeine can be building up your invisible load and unknowingly making it seem harder to cope.

> BEHIND THE SCENES, THE EFFECT OF CAFFEINE CAN BE BUILDING UP YOUR INVISIBLE LOAD AND UNKNOWINGLY MAKING IT SEEM HARDER TO COPE.

SUGAR

You know it's not good for you, but sometimes it feels like the only way you'll get through the afternoon is if you have something sweet. Even though you tell yourself you'll have only one biscuit, you end up eating more than you wanted to, and this makes you feel guilty and ashamed of what you see as your lack of discipline. You manage to talk yourself out of the downward spiral by vowing not to eat anything for afternoon tea tomorrow

Not everything that's faced can be changed, but nothing can be changed that is not faced.

JAMES BALDWIN

or by planning an extra gym session this week (but do you actually make it? And if you don't, how does this compound the guilt? And how heavy is this guilt in the backpack of your invisible load?).

ALCOHOL

You're so wired from the millions of demands of your day so to relax in the evening, you are drawn to alcohol. It feels like it's the only thing that will help you wind down. Maybe you drink too often, too much, or both. Alcohol is a depressant—that is how it acts on your nervous system. As a result, it makes everything feel like it is harder to cope with, even if that isn't the immediate effect you perceive when drinking; it might be adding in some rocks for you to carry around tomorrow. You might feel that the alcohol helps you nod off to sleep, but your sleep quality is compromised when alcohol has been consumed and, as a result, you find yourself needing coffee just to get through the day... and the cycle continues.

YOUR TIME

Your time seems to run faster than sand through an hourglass. Perhaps your email inbox feels like a time vortex where emails are never all dealt with or maybe you have more things on your to-do list than you have hours in the day. It feels impossible to reach the bottom of your inbox or end of your to-do list, and this bothers you.

YOU CAN'T SEE HOW YOU CAN MANAGE YOUR TIME, WITH ALL THAT'S NEEDED OF YOU, WITHOUT SETTING UP SUCH OVERWHELMING DAYS.

Or maybe you regularly have days when you have back-to-back meetings and appointments. You know you booked it in that way— you said yes to it all, but you can't see how you can manage each day with all that's needed of you without setting up such overwhelming days. This pace alone can contribute to your invisible load as you strive to keep up and get it all done.

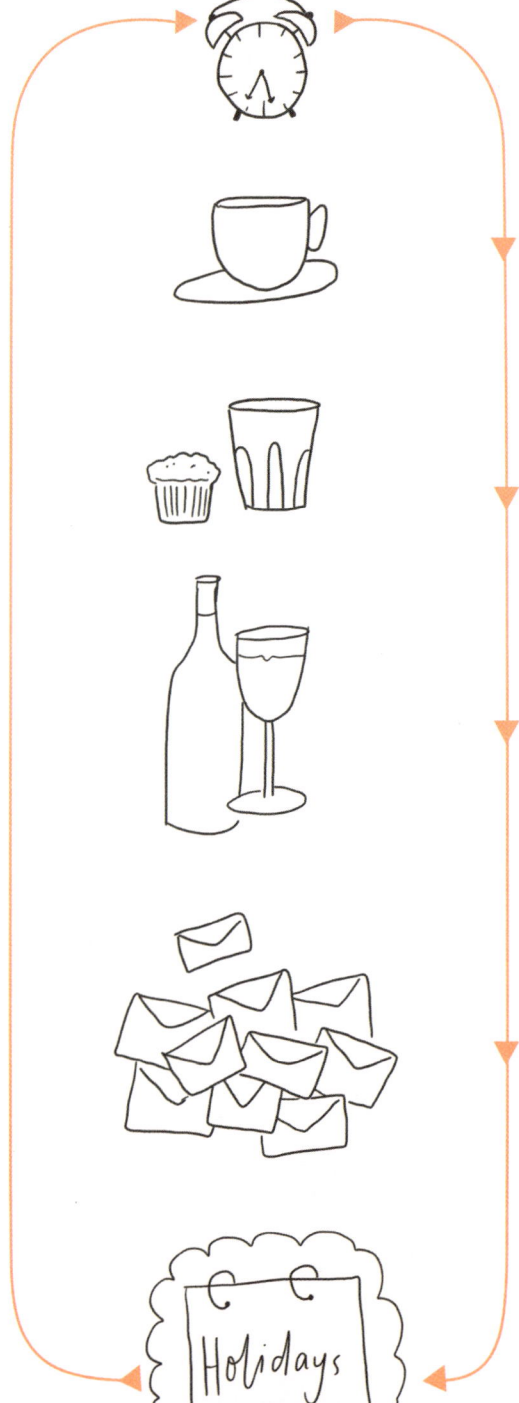

THE PEOPLE YOU CARE FOR

ALTHOUGH YOU LOVE TO HELP, YOU FEEL BURDENED BY YOUR RESPONSIBILITIES AND THE LACK OF FREEDOM YOU PERCEIVE THIS ENTAILS.

As time goes on, the number of people for whom you feel responsible—children, ageing parents, a friend who is struggling, work colleagues, clients, your boss who you feel puts enormous pressure on you—increases and although you love to help (or love the feeling of being needed), at times you feel burdened by your responsibilities and the lack of freedom you perceive this entails. There is a silent resentment eating away at you, amid the feeling of being overwhelmed, and this resentment can be a heavy load to carry.

Maybe you have children with food allergies in your home and you not only worry about their growth and development but you are exhausted from having to cook different meals. Or you might be raising your children solo and, after work and trying to do some exercise yourself each day, you are overwhelmed with what you face each evening. Meals, cleaning, homework, helping the children to find solutions to what they are experiencing, late-night emails to try to help you get ahead for the next day, washing, ironing, folding…

Or it might be that you've been in a long-term relationship and you know you can't stay because it will hurt your soul, although the thought of unpacking a whole life built together feels like too much to handle so you stay—yet it keeps eating away at you.

YOUR PHYSICAL BODY

Then there is your body. You may not share your concern with anyone, or perhaps just your closest girlfriends, but you are worried about your appearance. You feel like what you've always done to 'sort it' no longer works. It's not so much do I look 'good' or 'desirable' these days, but more along the lines of 'I wish I looked even half okay' or 'I wish I appreciated myself more 20 years ago instead of all the harsh judgement I put myself through'. There can be a sadness or regret that goes alongside this.

You have a bloated tummy each afternoon and/or evening, which saddens or frustrates you and sometimes translates in your head to self-talk that says, 'I'm fat'. This doesn't just affect your self-image and self-esteem but has a potential impact on intimacy if you have a partner. There can be flow-on effects and relationship strain, if this is something that has broken down.

YOUR ENVIRONMENT AND SEX HORMONES

Perhaps unknowingly, you eat or absorb too much environmental estrogen and substances that mimic estrogen from personal care and household cleaning products as well as pesticides, insecticides and herbicides from conventionally grown food.

TIPPING YOUR SEX HORMONE BALANCE CAN CAUSE YOU TO FEEL TERRIBLE.

This silent overwhelm can have an immense impact on your physical invisible load, particularly on the detoxification systems of your body and your sex hormone balance.

Tipping your sex hormone balance can cause you to feel terrible. For example, when there is too much estrogen and not enough progesterone in the lead-up to your period, you get irritable from excess estrogen and anxious from low progesterone, and this scenario alone can lead to significant feelings of being overwhelmed—regardless of what else you have going on in your world.

A similar feeling of overwhelm can occur in those women who are peri- or post-menopausal from excess heat or sleeplessness, as well as unpredictable anxious feelings, which can all stem from your sex hormone picture.

YOUR BELIEFS

Your beliefs can add a heavy weight to your invisible load. Perhaps, unconsciously, you seek validation and acknowledgement of your worth by sacrificing yourself and your needs and ways for others. You believe you must always put others first and be loving and unselfish to ensure you are loved, quite often living by an adage taught to you by your (well-meaning or otherwise) parents or guardians. You may

Deep in your heart you wish for a simpler life, or life how it once was before you unknowingly took on this invisible load.

DR LIBBY

also be continuing to seek their approval and/or love, whether they have passed away or are still alive. If you do something out of love it energises you, whereas if you do it out of duty it depletes you, and you end up resenting the activity or those involved. You also drive your invisible load further by trying to keep this anger and resentment under wraps.

GUILT

Then there's the guilt at not spending enough time with people you love—children, your partner, ageing parents, dear friends—because of too much work or too many tasks, or simply just wanting a moment to yourself. By now, you may be regularly too irritated with your partner to want to sit on the couch and hold hands while you watch a TV show you both enjoy. It's what you want—it just seems impossible to reach.

Deep in your heart you wish for a simpler life, or life how it once was before you unknowingly took on this invisible load, or you yearn for how it used to be with your partner before all of the duties of life took over. But how can you justify sitting on the couch when you could get more done? There are emails to reply to, washing to fold…yet your phone now tells you that you spend four hours a week on social media.

Or it might be that a relationship you once treasured ended, so although you immerse yourself in work after hours, you feel somehow inadequate (you're not) or you might silently tell yourself you are a failure (you're not) night after night on your own.

You regularly feel guilty about how you communicate with the people you love the most in the world—you're snappy, impatient, intolerant, easily frustrated, easy to anger. Some days you regret

how you've spoken to someone. You feel overwhelmed at times by your own responses and behaviour and you wonder where your old self has gone. This also makes you sad.

You notice that you go through periods where you wish your life away—busting for it to be the weekend or waiting for that two-week holiday you will take in six months. In the meantime, you keep missing what is actually your precious life.

YOUR OBLIGATIONS

You recognise that you need more time for yourself or to do things with your children or to exercise or cook, but you feel like you have to keep working these hours to pay your mortgage. Or perhaps you don't have a mortgage and the thought of one overwhelms you as you already have debt from car loans, personal loans, credit cards and your education. So even though the idea of a mortgage is too much for you, you are overwhelmed at the thought that you might never be able to buy a home. How do you take a step in another direction while you carry around the weight of these thoughts?

YOU CAN'T PUT YOUR FINGER ON IT, BUT YOU USED TO BE CLEARER ABOUT WHO YOU ARE AND WHAT MATTERED TO YOU.

A FEELING OF INCONGRUENCY

You can't put your finger on it, but you used to be clearer about who you are and what mattered to you. You're not even sure you know what you like any more. It is as if you are now living, or trying to live, inside someone else's values—your partner's, your parents', your flatmate's or those of your boss. And it feels like something just doesn't quite fit. Perhaps they value efficiency while you value contemplation, creativity and consideration, which is slower, so you give up how you like to live or work to fit in and please someone else.

It may not occur to you that one reason you feel ruffled and overwhelmed daily is from living in a way that is incongruent with your values. Or perhaps you've never even considered what your values are (more on this on page 251). At times when the burden of being overwhelmed has been constant for a while, you wonder: is this all there is? It was never supposed to be this way, yet you feel helpless to change it.

You worry constantly that you're not doing it right—this thing called life, which comes with no guidebook. That no matter where you are or what you're doing, it's never going to be enough. You want so badly to succeed and feel happy and for everyone around you to be happy, but you regularly feel like you have no idea what you're doing and every which way you turn you just seem to keep making (what you perceive are) more mistakes.

Yet trust that you cannot get it wrong.

Trust that whatever you choose is the right path for you. That you cannot get it wrong. Pause for a minute and really let that sink in. You cannot get it wrong. Sure, there are consequences to every decision. Some consequences you enjoy, others you don't. But whatever they are, they are meant for you and the unique experience of your soul, to foster her growth and full expression. Listen to your own inner knowing and do your best to live congruently with this. We'll unpack some of these rocks throughout these pages and while we do, see if you can start to see things that you find challenging—rather than them being 'in the way', do your best to see them as 'on the way'— as part of your experience while you get your turn on Earth.

Are you the Rememberer?

The weight of being in the memory seat

Most people in the world feel some form of pressure. There are likely degrees of it, and we can only know our own and the load that we each carry—you can't know the full extent of the load another carries. However, in most organised groups—families and businesses, for example—there is typically someone who is the 'Rememberer' of most of the details. [1] They are the one who carries the invisible load. The others (knowingly or unknowingly) tend to passively wait for directions. With all the remembering and foreseeing the Rememberer does, there tends to come a sense of immense responsibility. The classic internal statement of those carrying an invisible load is 'if I don't do it, it won't get done'. The others exclaim, 'I would have helped if only you'd asked'.

The Rememberer is always trying to share, take on and be responsible for everyone else's load, as well as their own, while those who wait for instructions (the Responders) tend to work in a silo. They will both often do a huge amount in a day and feel immense pressure, but for a Responder, it's usually their own work, not the details and tasks that keep the lives of others running smoothly on top of their own responsibilities—as the Rememberer does. Everyone means well.

The invisible load carrier tends to not ask for help because they believe it's just faster for them to do it themselves, instead of having to ask and explain and remind. And probably remind again. With all the energy—mental and physical—as well as the time it takes to explain it all, they would have had it done. The Rememberer coordinates and feels responsible for the moving parts of the family or business to ensure it all runs smoothly.

In certain areas of life (work, for example) someone might be a Rememberer, while in other areas (perhaps at home), they wait for directions. Yet I know more and more women who are the Rememberers in all domains, trying to foresee the major and minor discomforts that might come if balls get dropped. And they didn't necessarily sign up to carry these invisible loads in all life departments.

The load a Rememberer carries feels, at times, immense to them and a burden they wish they could have some relief from. But they can't take a break because they feel like it would all fall apart if they did. Plus, because the load they carry is invisible—there's not a list or a run sheet to work from, it's all about the little (and large) things in their head—they don't see how they could take a month off from the remembering duties. So, it all feels relentless.

THE LOAD THEY CARRY IS INVISIBLE— THERE'S NOT A LIST OR A RUN SHEET TO WORK FROM, IT'S ALL IN THEIR HEAD.

If you resonate with being the Rememberer in the groups you are part of, take small (or large!) steps towards delegating some tasks, and teach others what you know they could handle. From a teenager being given the job of cooking a family meal one night a week, to a staff member taking on the responsibility for correcting the spelling errors that you've been fixing in the board reports at work (among a million other tasks), look for opportunities to delegate and educate so your invisible task load starts to decrease. In other words, look for ways to share your load.

The Rememberer is always
trying to share, take on
and be responsible for
everyone else's load.

DR LIBBY

Racing to keep up

Can the body and mind handle the pace?

We live in a world in which many of us feel completely lost if we forget our smartphone for a day. We have become so accustomed to having everything at our fingertips that we get irritated with (or concerned about) a friend, partner—or even a business—if we don't hear back from them at warp speed. The internet means we have access to all kinds of information that was once available only in books and we spend much of our day staring at a screen.

As far as depicting humans living in the Western world today, it's perhaps fitting to show them with octopus arms, juggling their endless tasks, trying to get back to everyone who has contacted them via their home phone, office phone, mobile phone, email address 1, email address 2, email address 3, private messages on Facebook, Twitter, Instagram, Snapchat and likely numerous other mediums.

But, it wasn't all that long ago that we had no email, no instant messaging, no texting, no internet. Before the 90s, when these technologies became more widespread, the quickest way to shoot a document through to someone in a business was via fax (homes didn't tend to have them); otherwise we had the postal service and before faxes, pretty much only the post. If we left the house or our place of employment, we were uncontactable until we returned. Really think about that—no one could get hold of us unless we were at a home or business with a telephone.

Being in constant contact is a factor today in many situations where we feel the pressure of our invisible load. And can the body and mind really keep up with this pace?

Before we answer that, let's take another step back, and look specifically at changes happening for women. The 1960s saw the release of the combined oral contraceptive pill (OCP), which works by stopping the pituitary signalling the ovaries to ovulate. One thing that can be said is that it has played a pivotal role in giving women more choice regarding when they might have a family and it has opened up greater opportunities for pursuing further education and careers. However, the negative health effects some women experience from taking it are significant.

The OCP marked the beginning of women having control over their fertility, and the 1960s and 1970s saw women's wider involvement in many spheres wonderfully broaden. In 1979, the world witnessed the first female head of a global power with Margaret Thatcher becoming prime minister of England—which would probably have been scoffed at even 40 years prior.

In the 1930s and 1940s, around the time of World War II, most humans in the Western world were simply focused on surviving. They weren't worried about how they were living—they were simply hoping to meet their daily needs. It was also around this time that the chemical 'revolution' kicked off, with the first commercial pesticide being released in the 1940s. Synthetic herbicides and pesticides were beginning to be used on food consumed by both humans and animals. We now know that some of these compounds contain substances that mimic estrogen inside our body. To put that in perspective, it has only been in the last 80 years (just a couple of generations) that our food—the source of our nourishment—has radically changed. The change hasn't just been the introduction of synthetic chemicals, however; it has also been the continued and extensive industrialisation of food— when more and more food began to be refined and packaged up for us—which predominantly kicked off at the end of the war.

> IT HAS ONLY BEEN IN THE LAST 80 YEARS THAT OUR FOOD HAS RADICALLY CHANGED.

This is an important point in our evolutionary history because up until this time, we had simply eaten food, not junk. Plus, what is now referred to as 'food' is actually sprayed with pesticides but not labelled as such, so it seems odd to me that in modern times we have to stipulate when a food is 'organic'. Only a few generations ago, that was all there was. The ingestion of pesticides and junk are still very new to our bodies and the impact that this change in our food chain has had on our bodies and our health (not to mention the environment) cannot be overstated. Even more so when you consider that 80 years in evolutionary terms is just a tiny dot on the page in an entire book.

Another dot (perhaps more of a dash) in our evolutionary book, the Industrial Revolution, began around 250 years ago. It's important to note because up until this point in history, societies altered only gradually and there were many generations where almost nothing changed. The way great-grandparents grew up and lived was no different to how the youngest generation lived. But with the advent of machines, manufacturing, processing and the factory system, and a move away from handmade everything, a period of rapid change was initiated, never seen before in all of human history. And, of course, the technological revolution has sped everything up rapidly since then.

So, what did it look like before this warp speed shift? Well, there was still development and social evolution, but it was much slower. We went from being hunter-gatherers who lived in groups or tribes to the establishment of agriculture and the subsequent formation of cities. The first city was only established 4,600 years ago! [1] But all these developments spanned over thousands and thousands and thousands of years rather than a measly two hundred. And over these thousands of years, the human body gradually evolved into what it is today.

At the heart of biological evolution is survival: genetic variations and mutations, as well as natural selection, have resulted in differing traits being carried forward in individuals. The people with favourable characteristics for the changing environment are able to survive and reproduce and pass on those genes. Adaptation has been (and continues to be)

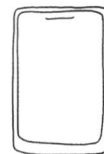

The
OLD BRAIN

The
NEW BRAIN

highly beneficial to survival. As such, behaviours and processes have been hard-wired into our brains that have allowed us to continue.

Over many eons, we have rewired some of what we've inherited and, of course, we've added to it greatly. However, much of that original, ancestral brain—the one that spanned the fork in the evolutionary road some five to seven million years ago which marked the beginning of various human species, leading to the rise of our species, *Homo sapiens*, some 300,000 years ago—is still there. It's just that now we've grown more brain around it.

OUR MODERN BRAIN

Here's a useful way to think about our modern brain. We have two thought systems. You might like to think of them as old and new, or reptilian and adapted—for now, I will refer to them as Old Brain and New Brain. The former is rapid, emotional and intuitive (with 'intuitive' in this instance meaning a reactive, instantaneous processing that occurs based on prior experience about what kept us safe), while the latter is much slower, and able to calculate and rationalise. The New Brain doesn't automatically examine the Old Brain and understand why it does what it does. New Brain doesn't usually even know that Old Brain has made a decision! Which is where a significant amount of our stress comes from today. More about this later.

The Old Brain has a style of wiring that was laid down across the millions of years of our history to help us survive. That still runs much of the show today, whether we choose for this to be the case or not. This part of our brain and the thought system it generates is constantly alert to danger and is always scouting out for potential situations that may threaten our lives. Our New Brain can see and learn and understand how things have changed so rapidly. Yet, our Old Brain is busy creating meanings from the situations we are involved with in an attempt to keep us safe. The problem is, the meanings are made up. They're not fact. Plus, it takes New Brain a very long time to (or it may never) peer inside Old Brain and see why on earth, when we are leaving work, all was well in the world and then within 30 minutes of arriving home we want to empty the contents of the pantry into our stomach.

So much of our stress today is derived from the lack of understanding between these two thought systems. We have not yet evolved for them to find common ground or to start to rewire ourselves away from some of the outdated survival patterns. And that's part of the challenge for our physical bodies when the world around us evolves so rapidly. The old wiring cannot adapt at such a rapid pace to understand what is actually going on.

SO MUCH OF OUR STRESS TODAY IS DERIVED FROM THE LACK OF UNDERSTANDING BETWEEN OUR TWO THOUGHT SYSTEMS.

SO WHY IS OUR BODY RESPONDING WITH STRESS?

If you wrote a book so that the proportional aspects of our evolution could be quantified, 200 pages would be dedicated to the nomadic hunter-gatherers' way of life, one page would cover agrarian societies and the last two centuries—our modern world—would be done in one brief paragraph at the end. [1]

To offer you additional visualisation options for just how little time we have undergone phantasmagorically large change, consider this: imagine a 30-centimetre school ruler, and allow that to represent the time we currently understand that we, as a species, have been on the planet—about 300,000 years. That means 1 millimetre, the smallest unit you can see on the ruler, represents 1,000 years. Using this time model, the last 100 years would not even be the size of a tiny dot left by a pin prick. And you would not even be able to see the past 30 years, but so much has changed and so rapidly. Yet it has taken our brain millions of years to evolve to be what it is today. It cannot now keep up with such lightning-fast change and adapt with haste. So we have to do our best to reassure this prehistoric aspect of ourselves that we are indeed safe when our relentless stress hormone production is telling every cell in our body otherwise.

Our bodies are bucking because they have not yet adapted (will they ever?) to not just what goes inside via what we eat, drink, breathe and put on our skin, but to the amount of information we are exposed to, the number of decisions we need to make each day, always being contactable, exposing our eyes to bright light from screens well into each evening, constantly comparing ourselves to others in such an accessible way… the weight of our invisible load is seemingly endless.

One of the ways the body is rebelling is with stress-related symptoms. It's trying to get your attention and alert you to necessary change or encouraging you to learn to accept what is happening. Initially, those symptoms tend to whisper their messages—you're more tired these days so go to bed earlier, or your digestion isn't what it used to be so you regularly experience bloating or other tummy troubles. The problems really begin when you don't heed those initial warnings. Eventually, your body will start shouting, usually in ways that you cannot ignore.

SAFETY

How our body responds to our lives is ultimately linked to our Old Brain. Stress stems from a lack of safety or a perception or concern that there is a risk that safety might be lost. To your body, it makes zero difference if any of that is real or perceived. A lack of safety can be physical (there's a burglar in my home) or emotional ('I don't feel safe in my relationship with my partner when they go quiet and stop talking to me, or raise their voice when they speak to me, as it triggers a fear that they'll leave', for example).

The challenge is, we need our old thought system—our super-speed, instantaneous, rapid processing of information, the reptilian Old Brain—when there is a physical threat. And we need our new thought system—the more rational, logical and lateral-thinking brain—to consider what might be going on for our partner when they go quiet. It's possible that they have a lot on their mind due to everything happening in their life and it has nothing to do with us. Yet Old Brain usually generates the first response in the relationship scenario—the one where we jump to the conclusion that it's something we've done and get worried about what it means for our relationship.

We then *might* try to analyse it later with New Brain, but most people live as if the meaning created by the Old Brain is literal. They don't stop to consider its accuracy or lack of it. In fact, you usually

can't even see that the Old Brain has dreamt something up—and if you can, it feels real. Which is why it can be very challenging, with our brains the way they are right now at this stage in human evolution, to answer the question—why do you do what you do, even though you know what you know? But I'll attempt to show you within these pages.

SO MUCH OF YOUR STRESS COMES FROM WHAT YOU DO WHEN YOU HAVE NO IDEA HOW ON EARTH YOU ENDED UP DOING WHAT YOU DID.

And yet, conversely, so much of your stress comes from what you do when you have no idea how on earth you ended up doing what you did. What led you to eat the whole packet of biscuits instead of just two? What led you to say yes yet again to help another person when you are drowning in your own tasks? How could you be utterly fine this morning and this afternoon feel flooded with anxious feelings? What led you into such a downward spiral with your mood when nothing major seems to have happened?

The reasons behind all of these scenarios can be biochemical, nutritional or emotional, or a combination of all three, which is why they are the pillars of every ounce of the work that I do. Each contributes to your invisible load. However, coming to know our brains and thought systems—for they, after all, drive the biochemistry and the nutritional choices—and truly understanding both sides, both systems, in my opinion, must be the next stage in our evolution. And that excites me tremendously.

EVOLVE, OR GO HOME

We are crazy if we think that our species will remain as it is forever. We will either evolve or become extinct. If you are not growing, you are dying. We can't remain as we are and each generation does its best to adapt, even if ever so slightly, to be better equipped to deal with the environment we find ourselves in. Perhaps through the production of new digestive enzymes in an attempt to better handle new substances in the food supply, for example.

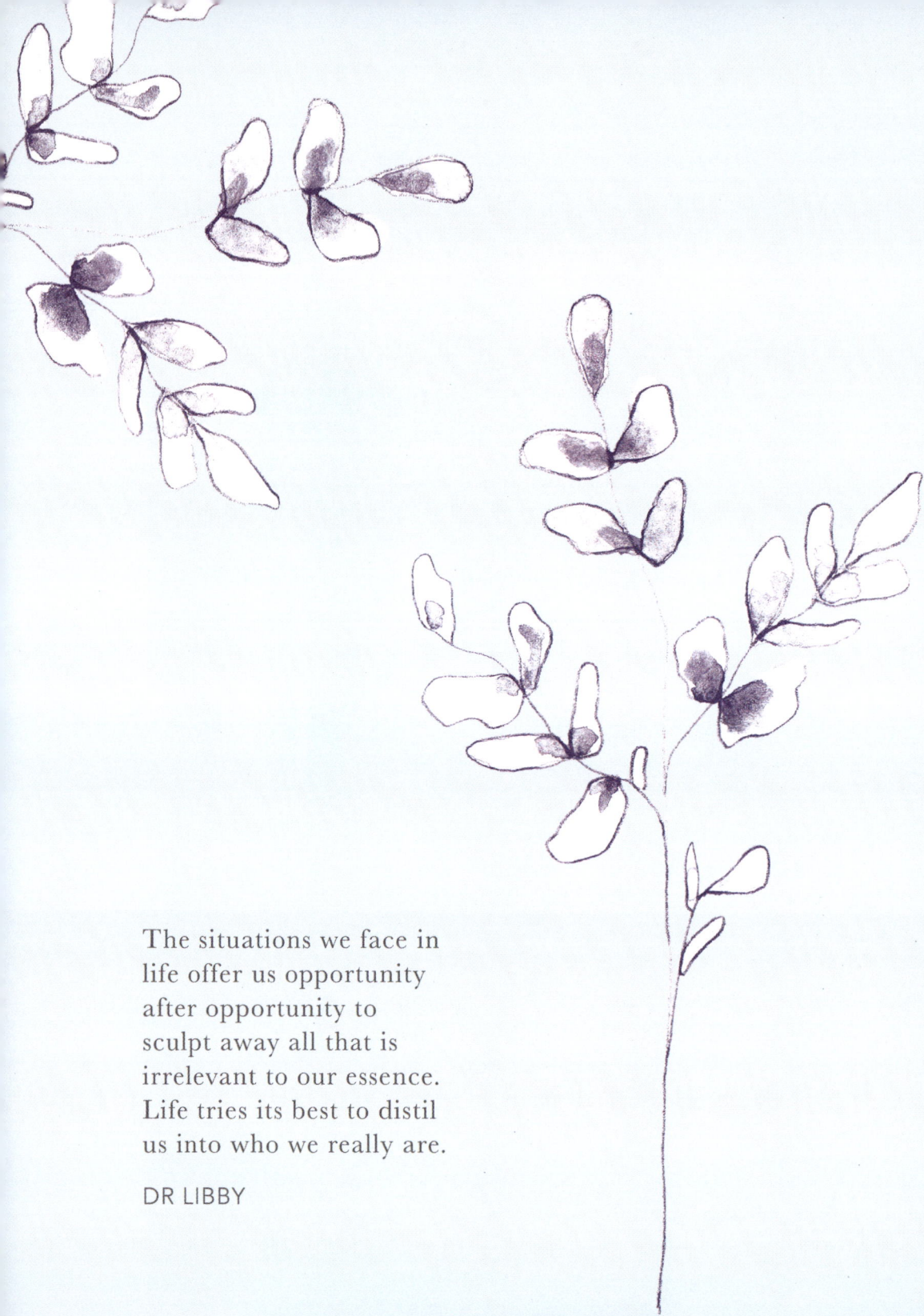

The situations we face in
life offer us opportunity
after opportunity to
sculpt away all that is
irrelevant to our essence.
Life tries its best to distil
us into who we really are.

DR LIBBY

But the path of evolution essential for our survival on Earth and for the progression of our species is one where consciousness rises. With less fear and Old Brain responses running the show. With greater awareness of the impact of our choices on everything beyond the end of our own noses. Especially if we insist on living our lives at this incredibly fast pace. And especially if we want Earth to remain as our home.

It is essential we come to learn how we think and be responsible for correcting the meanings Old Brain makes, because not examining and understanding ourselves in this way is what leads us to make all the choices that we typically later regret, despite knowing better.

These are the choices that lead us to judge ourselves and speak harshly to ourselves (and often others), which just leads us further down the rabbit hole filled with lousy self-worth and poor-quality lifestyle choices. Being able to truly see our Old Brain responses changes everything, and I am full of hope that, as a species, this will be our next evolutionary step.

BODY
LOAD

Having explored your load, let's now look at the ways that stress hormones impact your biochemistry and the ripple effect this has on other organs and body systems. The body is incredibly resilient and it may quietly cope with your load for a number of years. Yet slowly, over time, troubling symptoms can begin to unfold that indicate something isn't quite right. To you, they may seem to come out of nowhere, but they are your body crying out a little louder for your attention. These symptoms can tell us a lot about how your body is truly handling your invisible load. So, again, let's leave judgement at the door and simply try to understand what your body might be trying to tell you.

How thoughts become stress

Where it all starts

Have you ever wondered how your body takes a thought—or several thoughts in a row—or a momentary experience and turns them into stress?

How does your body really take the endless list of tasks you have in your mind, which no one else sees and that you wonder how you'll get done, and turn these thoughts into stress hormones? They're just tasks, after all—your life isn't actually in danger.

Imagine you're heading out the door to continue your day, after a frantic morning of meeting everyone else's needs—breakfasts, missing shoes, high-pressure dressing too close to departure time, collating everything you need to take with you for your day ahead. Just before you bundle everyone into the car (or perhaps you're on your own and about to make a dash for the train), you check your emails on your phone. The contents of that email shocks you and, in an instant, you notice that your heart, already racing from your chaotic morning, steps up a few notches and your breath catches in your chest. You're now fretting and the noise inside the car/train from the chatter and bickering seems cacophonous. Inside your head you're trying to devise a plan about how to respond to the email, but you're finding it hard to think clearly with all of the noise. You know you can't really deal with the email until you get to work, but you can't stop looping the issues it has raised in your mind.

Understanding what occurs physically in our bodies when we get stressed can go some way towards helping us alter our choices, responses, behaviours and perceptions. Appreciating just how hard our body works to keep us safe and healthy can sometimes spur us on when it comes to living in a way that is more supportive of our health, rather than just repeatedly hearing how bad stress is for us and feeling powerless to do anything to change that.

Stress hormones themselves—namely adrenaline and cortisol—are produced by the adrenal glands, walnut-sized structures that sit on top of our kidneys. But to understand their function and the impact of the stress hormones themselves, we first need to take a step back and consider what leads the adrenals to be on the receiving end of signals that instruct them to produce adrenaline and cortisol.

Put simply, stress hormones are not just randomly produced. The adrenals or the nervous system must receive a message from another part of you that has assessed the information available in your internal and external environments. This information might involve seeing what nutrients are present or missing from your blood (remembering that missing nutrients means famine to the body, not that you have access to plenty of food but have been relying way too much on takeaways in the recent past because you're time poor, or that you have voluntarily gone on a restrictive diet), sex hormone information (involved in whether you ovulate regularly or not, as one example), and the effects of your perceptions or reality on whether there is more fear or love.

STRESS HORMONES THEMSELVES–NAMELY ADRENALINE AND CORTISOL–ARE PRODUCED BY THE ADRENAL GLANDS, WALNUT-SIZED STRUCTURES THAT SIT ON TOP OF OUR KIDNEYS.

It all starts in the brain, in a small region called the hypothalamus, which connects our nervous system to our endocrine (hormonal) system. One of the tasks of the hypothalamus is to assess our level of safety at all times. Essentially, it repeats the question 24/7: am I safe? To identify an answer it assesses you both biochemically (for example, how much adrenaline you might have zooming around in the bloodstream at the moment) and emotionally (such as if you felt that a passing comment from one of your colleagues meant they didn't think you did a good job, which can lead you to experience an emotional lack of safety with job security or your colleague's perception of you). You'll see more on this concept of 'safety' throughout the book.

If the answer to the hypothalamus's question of 'am I safe?' is no, which as you'll see throughout this book is predominantly the case for many people these days, the hypothalamus sends a message to the pituitary gland, also in the brain and often referred to as the mother gland, that you are not safe and that she needs to get to work to help keep you safe. So, it is the pituitary who then communicates the real or perceived lack of safety information to all of the other glands in the endocrine system. This includes the thyroid gland (in the neck), the adrenals, the ovaries in women and the testes in men. This all leads the adrenal glands to respond to the hormonal messages the pituitary sends—primarily adrenocorticotropic hormone (ACTH)—and they then produce stress hormones. The system involving the hypothalamus, pituitary and the adrenals is often referred to as the HPA axis.

The nervous system is also involved in awakening the adrenals to the 'threat' at hand. If they are on the receiving end of stimulation by what are called sympathetic preganglionic neurons—or put simply, the sympathetic nervous system (SNS)—this too can drive stress hormone production. The nerve endings of the SNS themselves can also release another stress hormone known as noradrenaline, whose actions are very similar to those of adrenaline.

So, what actually leads you to produce stress hormones and what do they do in your body?

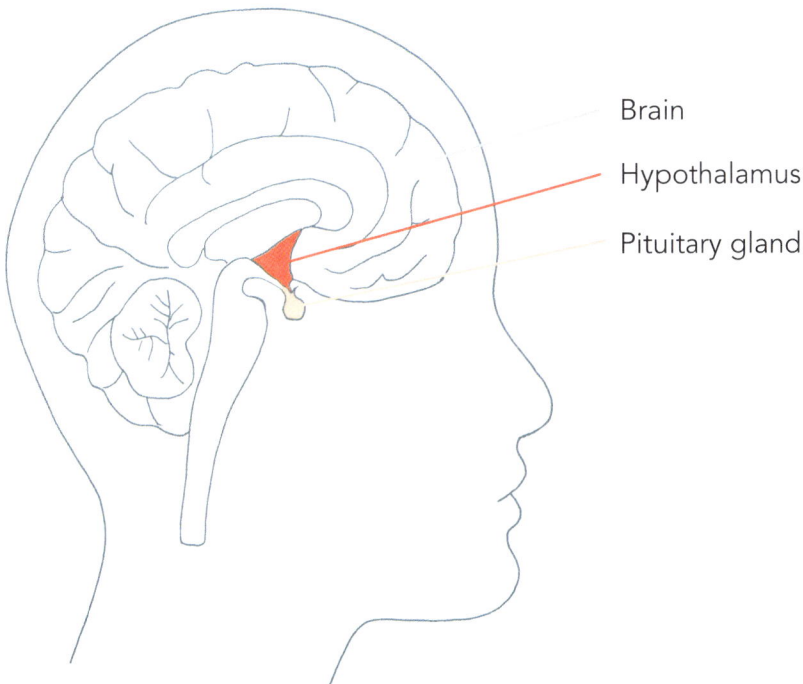

Brain

Hypothalamus

Pituitary gland

WHAT LEADS TO THE PRODUCTION OF STRESS HORMONES?

As you now know, signals from the pituitary gland and the SNS lead you to produce cortisol, adrenaline and noradrenaline. What specifically leads to this will be explored in detail throughout the book, but in a nutshell this can include:

- a genuine threat to your life, such as being involved in a natural disaster or a car driving out in front of you

- caffeine

- running long distances

- a perception of pressure

- a perception that everything needs to be dealt with urgently

- worrying about what other people think of us

- worrying about the infinite number of invisible tasks that you need to attend to, which no one else in your home thinks of

- worrying about finances, relationships, children, workload— worrying in general if it's persistent and continual

- and many other situations that we will explore throughout the book, including a frantic morning of juggling the needs of family members with what you need to do for yourself and work demands, described previously.

WHAT DO STRESS HORMONES DO?

There are two 'categories' of stress hormones: the first group, adrenaline and noradrenaline, are what we typically make in response to acute stress, while cortisol is made when the stress response has become chronic. Knowingly or unknowingly, for most people today, daily stresses are both acute and chronic in nature and levels of both groups are often relentlessly elevated (however, situations of long-standing chronic stress can eventually lead cortisol levels to become low, explained on page 67).

ADRENALINE AND NORADRENALINE

Stress hormones are designed to literally save your life. Historically, adrenaline was only produced when we were actually in danger. Today it is ironic that, although it can still save our lives (when, say, a car drives out in front of you and you need to slam on your brakes), its constant and relentless production is burdening the body, rather than fostering relief.

STRESS HORMONES ARE DESIGNED TO LITERALLY SAVE YOUR LIFE.

Adrenaline is typically made in situations of acute stress, while noradrenaline will be made constantly in the background due to a low (or high!) level of activity in the sympathetic nervous system. For most people today, this is relatively and constantly elevated. Imagine how much our hectic morning lady made between waking and 8 a.m. And she will likely do this most days of the week and continue to do so as each day and night unfolds, incrementally adding to her own invisible load.

Adrenaline has many different actions depending on which cells it is acting on. All of them are designed to help increase your chance of survival, given the threat your body perceives you are under. For example, adrenaline might be acting on cells in the cardiovascular system, the kidneys (affecting urine output and fluid retention and much more) or the nervous system.

Its main actions include the following:

- **Increases blood pressure and heart rate** to help pump more oxygen-carrying blood and nutrients to your periphery (think the muscles in your arms and legs) to assist your escape. Yet you might just be sitting in your car having read an email that requires you to have a confronting conversation.

- **Enlarges the pupil of the eye**, which allows more light to enter, helping you see more clearly in potentially lower light. From a survival standpoint, this would help you to see approaching threats and potential routes of escape more clearly.

- **Mobilises glucose into the blood** (from stores known as glycogen in the liver and muscles), to give you a fast-burning fuel to help you escape, plus supply the brain with its preferred fuel. This can affect the efficiency with which you use body fat as a fuel and can also lead you to crave sugar to top up your glucose fuel tank. This will have been set up for our frantic morning lady in response to the first few hours of her day.

- **Diverts blood away from digestion** to the large muscles of the legs and buttocks, plus the arms. Digestion simply isn't a priority when your body is perceiving that your life is in danger and, as a result, it wouldn't be surprising if mid-afternoon (or constant) bloating is a challenge for our hectic morning lady.

- **Keeps you alert** or, when in excess, alarmed and on red alert. This can lead to living each day with intensity, having overwhelming anxious feelings, or overreacting to what unfolds, which affects you and everyone around you and stops you sleeping deeply and restoratively. It would not have been surprising if our frantic morning lady reacted with intensity to the noisy car after reading her email, later regretting her outburst, judging herself harshly for how she spoke to her precious young humans and disliking herself and who she thinks she has become—all in response to the excessive and relentless production of stress hormones.

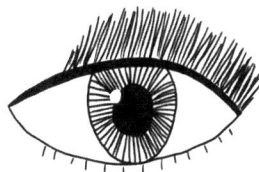

I want you to consider that if these things occurred just 10 times a year, of course the body would handle it. However, the way most people live these days means they are always in this state. Think that through. When you are almost always living with elevated levels of adrenaline, it puts you at risk for the longer-term consequences of these stress hormone-related changes that may contribute to daily dysfunction or disease for you.

For example:

- hypertension and cardiovascular diseases

- debilitating loss of eyesight (faster than age-related)

- Type 2 diabetes or hypoglycaemia;

- body fat increases that don't alter with changes in food intake or movement

- what feels like insurmountable, relentless sugar cravings

- irritable bowel syndrome (IBS), reflux or other gut-based illnesses

- relationship (all types of relationships) challenges and regretting the way you spoke to the people you love the most in the world, as well as colleagues and strangers, because of chronic (persistent) overreacting

- insomnia or chronic sleep problems

- feeling stressed all the time; daily anxious feelings; at times feeling like you can't cope.

INBOX OF DOOOM!!!

CORTISOL

Cortisol plays many positive roles in the body when you make it in the right amount at the right times of the day. When you make too much or too little, or your cortisol curve is high when it is supposed to be low, or vice versa, it can wreak havoc on your health, energy, inflammation, maintenance of muscle mass, blood glucose regulation, immune response and whether you use body fat effectively as a fuel. Adrenaline is supposed to be our acute stress hormone, while cortisol is made in higher than optimal amounts when stress has become chronic, which it has for most people in the Western world today.

Historically, the only long-term, commonly occurring stressors humans faced were scenarios like floods, famines and wars, during which food was typically scarce. These days we make cortisol when worrying about our relationships, finances, our health, the health concerns of a loved one—or anything else. When we do so, the body is on the receiving end of what elevated cortisol communicates, which is that there is no food left in the world. It therefore has a significant impact on metabolic rate and whether the body gets the message to store fat or burn it.

CORTISOL IS SUPPOSED TO BE NICE AND HIGH IN THE MORNING, WHICH GIVES YOU ENERGY AND VITALITY TO BOUNCE OUT OF BED.

Cortisol is supposed to be nice and high in the morning, which gives you energy and vitality to bounce out of bed. From there it gradually decreases across the day so that its levels are low by 10 p.m., allowing you to fall asleep and rest restoratively. But you'll see on page 66, where we look at the stages of stress, how cortisol levels alter with the length of time we experience stress. Since stress or being overwhelmed is a constant companion for people, cortisol is a significant contributing factor to their physical suffering. Most cells of the body have cortisol receptors, so its actions are widespread.

When it is produced in the ideal amounts, cortisol helps to:

- regulate inflammation in the body, as it is a powerful anti-inflammatory
- foster an appropriate and robust immune response
- manage blood glucose levels
- support good energy and vitality
- manage the salt water balance in the body, which also significantly influences blood pressure
- facilitate processes involved in having a good memory.

When it is in excess, cortisol:

- is catabolic, meaning it breaks down your muscles
- slows metabolic rate, as a result of the loss of muscle mass because muscle cells burn more energy than fat cells, hence body fat levels increase (particularly around our middle and on our back—the torso thickens)
- can disrupt the regulation of blood fats such as cholesterol and triglycerides
- can contribute to elevated blood glucose levels
- can interfere with good-quality sleep
- contributes to poor memory
- may lead to poorer gut health
- decreases libido.

When cortisol levels are too low, or if it is being used up too rapidly so not enough of it is available for other actions, some of the symptoms typically include:

- chronic, deep fatigue
- stiffness, which is usually worse on waking
- other conditions of inflammation being diagnosed
- chronic (often low-grade) infections
- other endocrine problems starting to occur such as thyroid problems (more about this in a later section).

A NOTE ON NUTRITION

Also consider what is needed to produce the actual structures of the stress hormones themselves. B vitamins, vitamin C and magnesium, for example, are used in the processes of creating stress hormones. The body prioritises what, when and where it uses everything, including these nutrients, all with your survival as its paramount focus. Therefore, the creation of stress hormones is very high in the ranking of importance. Trouble is, if you eat in a way that doesn't supply you with enough of these nutrients for the stressfully overwhelming period—or way of life—that you are living, you won't have the ingredients to make the cake. In other words, you will not be able to produce enough of the hormones, particularly cortisol, that your body is screaming at you to make.

It also means you won't have those nutrients available for other processes that need them, such as your immune response, cholesterol and other blood fat regulation, liver detoxification pathways, skin clarity and collagen production, great-quality fingernails and hair, or energy production for you to enjoy life. Poor nutrition and chronic stress are a debilitating combination, remembering that stress doesn't just come in the form of big, life-changing occurrences, but can come each morning, indeed each day and night just from how we live, what we need to tend to, the enormous invisible load that so many people today carry.

Consuming enough nutrients for your needs, as well as taking steps to ensure that your body gets the message that it doesn't need to produce copious amounts of stress hormones, are two vital ways we can make a major difference to our health now.

They will also go a long way towards preventing many lifestyle-related diseases from unfolding down the track. Remember, you want to live long and die short, not the other way around.

Breath and stress

The role of the nervous system

When we feel under pressure and overwhelmed, the nervous system has a significant part to play. If you've ever experienced that wired sensation, with the consequences of anxious feelings felt everywhere—think bloating and unpredictable bowel patterns, headaches out of nowhere, wide awake at 2 a.m., and an appetite you can't predict—this is your nervous system responding to the information it is receiving.

However, it's unlikely that you're aware of the type of information that is being sent and received among the millions of biochemical pathways happening inside you. You don't sit at your desk having just read the email that has sent you into a spin instructing your body to cope with all of this by making stress hormones. The nervous system picks up on your responses and does its best to support you. It is obtaining its information from your thoughts and perceptions ('there aren't enough hours in the day') as well as from your choices (all of this caffeine has my body's tension level high and my shoulders are up around my ears while I'm typing, for example).

Today in the Western world, compared to yesteryear, we are relatively safe from wartime stress, although tragically other forms of trauma and natural disasters can lead people to experience feelings of being unsafe. Yet too many people unknowingly tell their body, every minute of every waking hour, that they aren't safe, despite the fact that in that very moment they are. This latter scenario—where you are safe, but your body is getting the message that you aren't—is a significant aspect of the biochemistry of overwhelm and a huge contributing factor to your invisible load.

The key to unpacking this part of your invisible load starts with understanding your extraordinary nervous system. The nervous system is made up of the brain, spinal cord and all the nerves that govern interior processes. When the messages it sends and receives are in harmony it creates a magnificent symphony. However, for most people today, the nervous system orchestra spends most of its performance time rather raucous and out of tune, and the conductor seems to have lost the music sheets.

Our **central nervous system** (CNS), which comprises our brain and spinal cord, receives sensory information and responds accordingly. These responses are in the form of signals sent to other parts of your nervous system or to other parts of your body. You can 'instruct' yourself to type, pick up a glass of water and put it to your lips, and do squats at the gym, and signals will be sent from the CNS via the somatic division of the peripheral nervous system to your muscles, to allow you to do these things. In other words, your conscious, instructional, thinking mind allows you to control these processes.

The **autonomic nervous system** (ANS), on the other hand, is responsible for directing body processes that you cannot instruct, those not under conscious control. These include how rapidly your heart beats, how well your body digests a meal and healing a cut on your hand. The ANS has two parts: the sympathetic nervous system (SNS) and the parasympathetic nervous system (PNS), the former driving the stress response and the latter the calm response.

The **enteric nervous system** (ENS) is within the wall of the digestive tract, and with some help from the other parts of the nervous system, it governs gastrointestinal function. You might momentarily wonder what something related to digestion has to do with stress and overwhelm. Well, the ENS sends signals to the brain and the brain sends information back about what is occurring and how next to respond to that. You may notice that if you feel anxious or your mood is low or you feel overwhelmed, your desire for food varies. Or your satiety levels are different from when you are calm, or the function of your digestive system is altered and you experience some symptoms that don't occur when you are calm. You might notice irritable bowel-type symptoms, reflux, constipation, a sense of incomplete evacuation (that there is more waste to pass than is being eliminated), diarrhoea or bloating.

I cannot tell you the number of people who try to treat their IBS with food alone and this is of course an important and often necessary first step. But it is step one. Addressing the stress that is almost always involved is essential to completely resolving the symptoms (you can read more about how stress impacts digestion from page 119).

What I really want you to take away from this is that many aspects of the nervous system are involved in the stress response, which means every ounce of our physical structure can be affected by overwhelm.

EVERY OUNCE OF OUR PHYSICAL STRUCTURE CAN BE AFFECTED BY OVERWHELM.

It is the ANS that is most important to understand when it comes to overwhelming stress, though. While the somatic nervous system is controlled by your thinking, it is vital to note that you are unable to control the ANS by instructing it. It is regulated by your unconscious mind. This is the part of your brain that knows better than you and has your survival at its heart. Because you can't boss the ANS around, the only way you can influence it is via how you breathe. More on this in a moment, as it REALLY matters.

With the two branches of the ANS—the SNS and the PNS—the challenge for so many people with their health today is that they get stuck with the SNS switched on. I refer to this as SNS dominance.

When the SNS is constantly amped up, the organs, tissues and cells of the body receive a barrage of messages that a heightened level of activity is required and that there is, potentially, immediate danger. But as you now understand from previous pages, much of the basis of stress hormone production and SNS dominance today is due to our perceptions, not a genuine threat to our life. So, all of the substances inside of us that are mobilised to help us get out of there end up hurting us, taking away from our health and the quality of our lives.

For example, when you activate your SNS, blood pressure increases—one in five adults in New Zealand and Australia have high blood pressure. There are many mechanisms that drive this, but this is a major one. Additionally, the blood supply that is usually so efficient in supporting digestive system function gets diverted away from digestion to your periphery—to your arms and legs—to help you fight or flee from this danger you are supposedly in. One in five women in Australia have IBS, and rates are thought to be even higher for women in New Zealand (more on IBS on page 135). Food is playing a role in many people experiencing IBS, but so is this stress response.

Also—and for many of you this will be a significant learning from this book—the SNS changes the fuel that your body perceives is safe and efficient for you to use. In any given moment the body is making a decision about whether to use fat or glucose as a fuel. It is always a combination of both, but the ratios can shift. And one of the most potent factors that influences this is the arm of the ANS that is activated.

When your body is getting the message that your life is in danger (SNS activation), it needs to supply you with a fast burning fuel to power you to get out of danger. Take a wild guess which is your fast burning fuel—glucose or fat? Glucose is. So, your body will predominantly utilise glucose rather than body fat as a fuel when the SNS is activated. Conversely, we burn fat efficiently when the PNS is activated and for many people this is one of the missing pieces in their weight loss puzzle.

The image below highlights the various parts of the body that are stimulated by SNS and PNS activation.

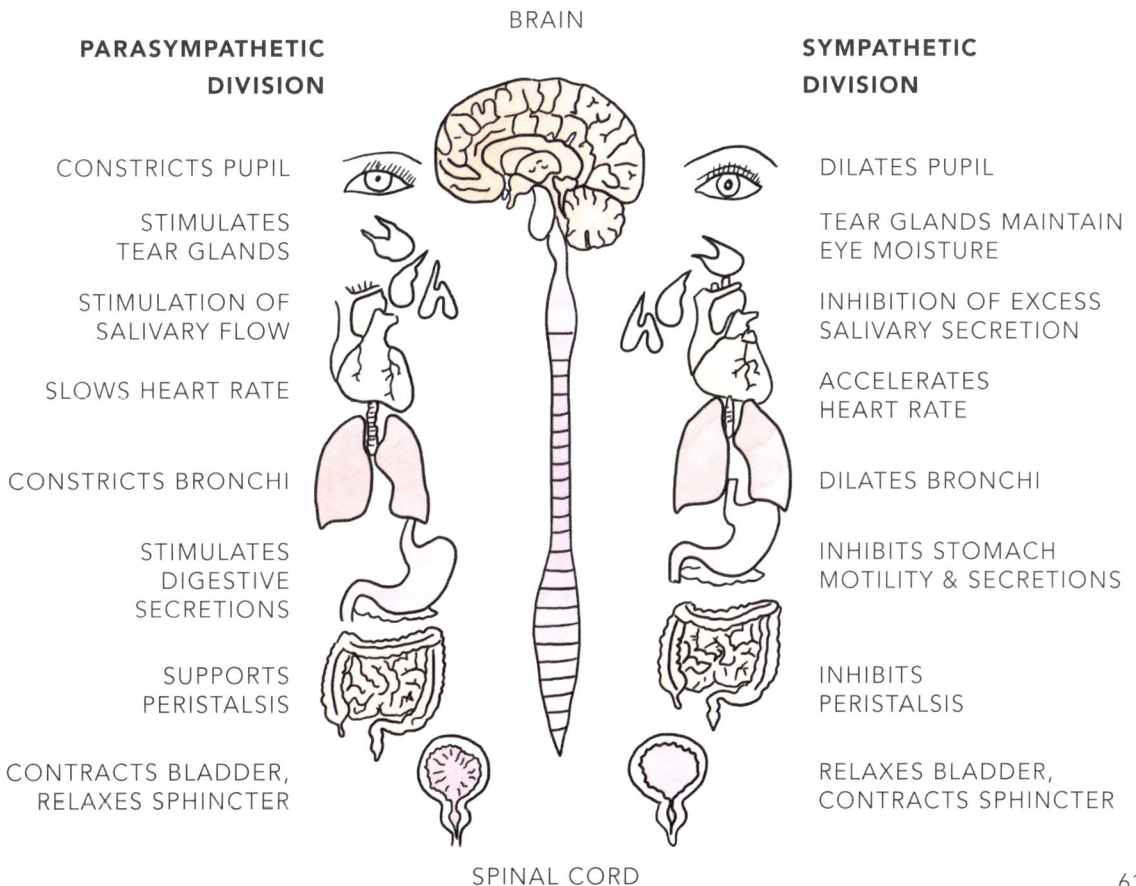

BRAIN

PARASYMPATHETIC DIVISION

SYMPATHETIC DIVISION

CONSTRICTS PUPIL — DILATES PUPIL

STIMULATES TEAR GLANDS — TEAR GLANDS MAINTAIN EYE MOISTURE

STIMULATION OF SALIVARY FLOW — INHIBITION OF EXCESS SALIVARY SECRETION

SLOWS HEART RATE — ACCELERATES HEART RATE

CONSTRICTS BRONCHI — DILATES BRONCHI

STIMULATES DIGESTIVE SECRETIONS — INHIBITS STOMACH MOTILITY & SECRETIONS

SUPPORTS PERISTALSIS — INHIBITS PERISTALSIS

CONTRACTS BLADDER, RELAXES SPHINCTER — RELAXES BLADDER, CONTRACTS SPHINCTER

SPINAL CORD

Essentially, when you are stressed or overwhelmed or simply living at a million miles an hour, forever in this switched-on state dealing with so much that only you see, the efficient functioning of everything is compromised. On top of this, continuing to recite or think about how stressed you are or mulling over your worries every day does nothing to help you produce fewer stress hormones and spend less time with the SNS activated.

Given that we can't instruct our ANS, and it is the way we breathe that can influence which arm's activity is heightened, let's explore it further. This goes some way to giving you practical steps to take to decrease stress hormone production and spend more time with the PNS activated, which helps to quell the overwhelm and offers some sense of relief.

THE WAY YOU BREATHE INFLUENCES YOUR CALM

When you breathe with short, sharp, shallow breaths, and it is the upper part of your chest that moves, the SNS is well and truly activated. It is adrenaline that is powerfully driving this style of breathing. So, even if you are simply sitting around a boardroom table or driving your car to buy groceries, your body is getting the message that your life is literally in danger. Really contemplate that.

When you breathe deeply and move your diaphragm, you inhale and your lower abdomen expands, then you exhale and your tummy shrinks back in towards your spine. When you breathe in this way you communicate to every cell in your body that you are safe. The reason for this? If your life was truly in danger, you would never breathe this way. You need the short, sharp, shallow breaths, the ripple effect of adrenaline production as well as SNS activation, to help you escape from a genuine threat to your life.

In as many moments as you can remember throughout your day, aim to take long, slow breaths. While this might seem small, it is tiny choices like these that will help your body to take some of the weight off your invisible load, one breath at a time.

WHEN YOU ARE OVERWHELMED
AND IN THIS SWITCHED-ON
STATE DEALING WITH SO MUCH
THAT ONLY YOU SEE, THE
EFFICIENT FUNCTIONING OF
EVERYTHING IS COMPROMISED.

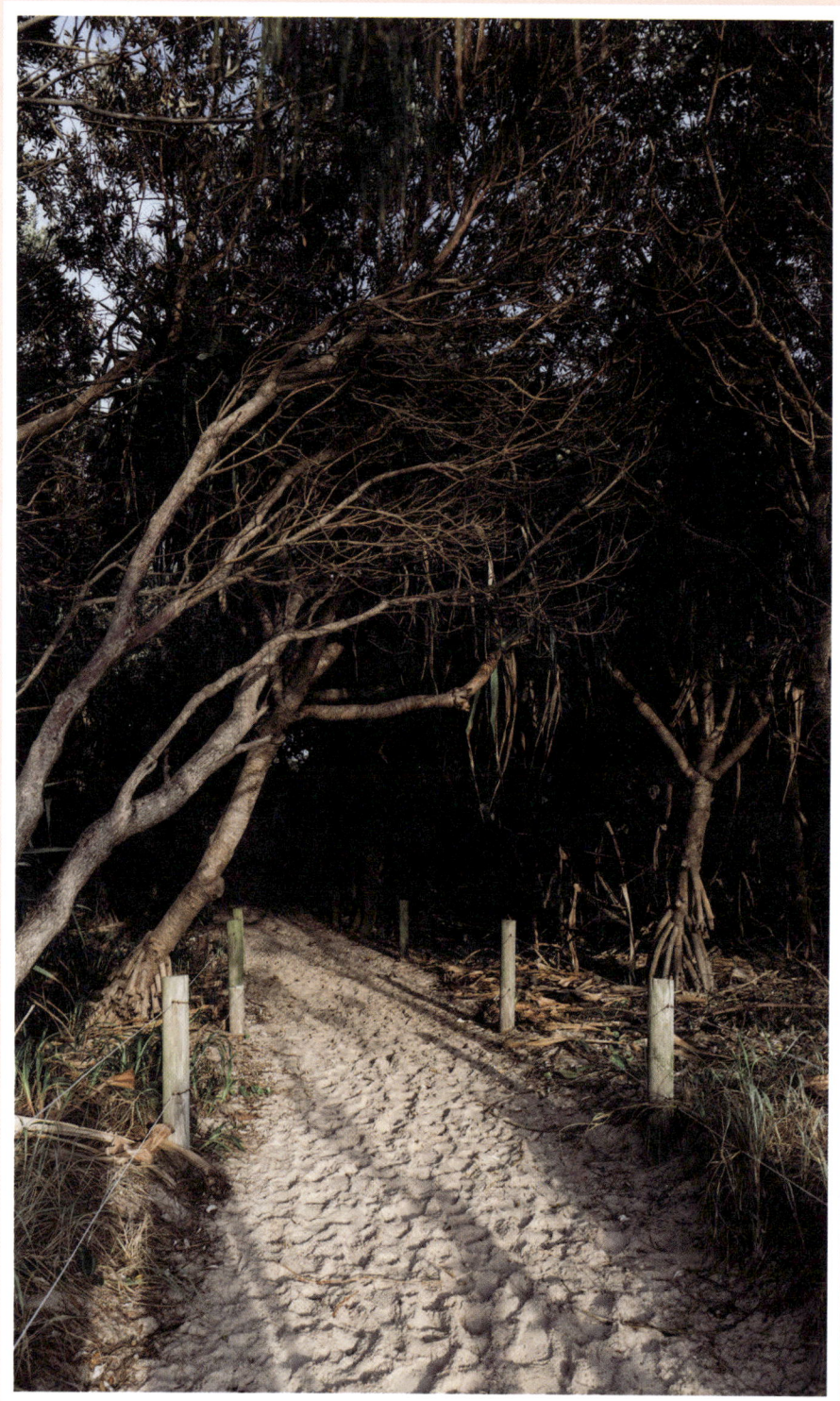

How we end up exhausted

Is all stress bad for us?

Not all stress is bad for us. Stress that supports our health is known as 'eustress'. Think of a male gymnast's physique. He didn't get that way from never stressing his body. He has those muscles because he puts them under repeated duress for periods of time so they grow in strength and size.

Eustress might also help us achieve goals with our chosen course of study or our career. The thing is, with eustress, we rest and we recover before the next stress comes, so we gradually adapt. This adaptation is called hormesis—it is an adaptive response to a moderate and usually intermittent stress. It is a process in which exposure to a 'low dose' of something that would be damaging at higher doses 'induces an adaptive, beneficial effect'. [1]

The way a hormone feels to you initially is uniquely yours, although there is certainly some commonality. There are those who seek the sensation of adrenaline and those who go out of their way to avoid it. Some people almost get addicted to the rush, while others stress out about getting stressed and stress out further with their desire for what feels like an unattainable calm. When you first make additional adrenaline, you might enjoy some of its benefits, such as sharper thinking, increased energy and a sensation of aliveness. This may prompt you knowingly or unknowingly to seek more of these perks.

Yet much of the stress we experience today is damaging because of its constant and relentless nature. The effects of adrenaline can easily move beyond these uplifting benefits, because adrenaline has a dose response—a threshold over which your experience of it becomes highly uncomfortable for your brain and your body. And you may not realise that what began as clearer thinking has added more weight to your invisible load, not only from the relentless stress hormone production but also its ripple effect on other organs and body systems.

So, to better understand what occurs as the stress response becomes prolonged, let's examine how stress can lead us to exhaustion.

While it might seem like you one day ended up in a pile of exhaustion, there are actually three stages to the stress response: the alarm phase, the high cortisol phase and then finally the inadequate cortisol phase which is where people commonly experience 'adrenal fatigue'.

1 STAGE 1: THE ALARM PHASE

During this phase, adrenaline is high. This is acute stress. If it is brought on by a balloon popping, the surge of adrenaline is short-lived and we return to what is called 'homeostasis', a state of equilibrium on the inside. The thing is, for most people, there might be the odd occasion when their adrenaline skyrockets due to a sudden loud noise, but mostly what drives adrenaline production today means it is constantly elevated: caffeine, the perception of pressure and urgency and worrying what other people will think of us because we are about to be late to a meeting, or because of what we said in a text message a few days ago, or due to a not-yet-sent and much delayed reply to their email, or due to the fact you haven't called them for over a week. The production of adrenaline these days is usually not in response to trying to save our lives; it is a by-product of our choices and thinking.

Historically, when adrenaline production was predominantly made as a result of a literal threat to our life, its period of time at an elevated level was brief. However, with the constantly high levels of adrenaline that occur for most people today comes myriad changes to our physiology, outlined thoroughly on page 51. So, because adrenaline elevates blood pressure, increases heart rate, disrupts digestion and leads you to burn predominantly glucose, not fat, as your fuel, inflammation increases. The body knows that too many inflammatory compounds are damaging and can shorten life (remember the body has survival as its heart). Therefore, after so long with elevated adrenaline, you move into the second stage of the stress response.

STAGE 2: HIGH CORTISOL PHASE

Stage 2 kicks in, in part, as an attempt to down-regulate inflammation, which is why the body's chronic stress hormone now increases its production. Hello high cortisol. You still haven't dealt with the high adrenaline level and what was driving that, and now you also have high cortisol. As you learnt on page 53, cortisol has many useful actions when we make it in the right amount. But when it increases, it can start to play havoc with the regulation of blood glucose, cholesterol and triglyceride (blood fat) levels. It also breaks down muscle which slows metabolic rate, so your clothes start to get tighter even though how you eat and move has not changed (explored in detail in my book *Accidentally Overweight* and my nine-week online course). Some people remain in this biochemical place for years or decades. For others, though, when the stress response has gone on for too long, they enter the third stage of the stress response.

STAGE 3: INADEQUATE CORTISOL PHASE

In this stage, there are two possible scenarios that could lead to the symptoms of what appears as 'low cortisol', the main symptoms being a deep, unrelenting fatigue, and body pain and stiffness that is worse in the mornings. Scenario one is that the body can no longer respond to the endless, demanding barrage of signals that keep being sent by the pituitary to the adrenals to produce the cortisol necessary to deal with the stress the person is either perceiving or experiencing. Morning waking cortisol and, for some, cortisol levels across the whole day might be low.

Scenario two occurs when you are still able to produce cortisol but you cannot produce enough to keep putting out the inflammatory fires created by the adrenaline you've never dealt with. So, there's no problem with your ability to produce it, but it doesn't meet demands. As such, you experience the same symptoms as if your cortisol levels are too low because you are metabolising what you are producing so rapidly.

Stage 3 is sometimes referred to as 'adrenal fatigue'. Another term that is usually more helpful than this is HPA axis dysregulation, even though it is a bit of a mouthful! This reminds us that when you have been on red alert for so long that you end up with stage 3 symptoms, it won't just be your adrenals that need support. Usually by now you also have symptoms that relate to the nervous system and other endocrine glands, remembering that these are all under the control of the hypothalamus and the pituitary gland: the thyroid, the ovaries (reproductive system and sex hormones) and aspects of digestion, blood glucose regulation and insulin production.

THE PRODUCTION OF ADRENALINE THESE DAYS IS USUALLY NOT IN RESPONSE TO TRYING TO SAVE OUR LIVES; IT IS A BY-PRODUCT OF OUR CHOICES AND *THINKING*.

We can go a long way to helping someone recover from stage 3 stress with dietary changes, herbal medicine and breath-focused practices, but the most effective and long-term, sustained improvements occur when we get to the heart of what the stress is really all about and turn off the tap through changes in actions and/ or thinking, or simple acceptance. Or, at the least, if we can return to a state where the stress is intermittent and there are periods of rest and recovery, we experience periods of eustress and the adaptation and growth that offers.

The consequences of stress

Signs to look for in your body

Stress hormones drive their own symptoms that you might experience. They can also interfere with the production and/or regulation of other organs and systems inside you. Many of them overlap. Here's a snapshot of some of the signs to look for that can be consequences of stress.

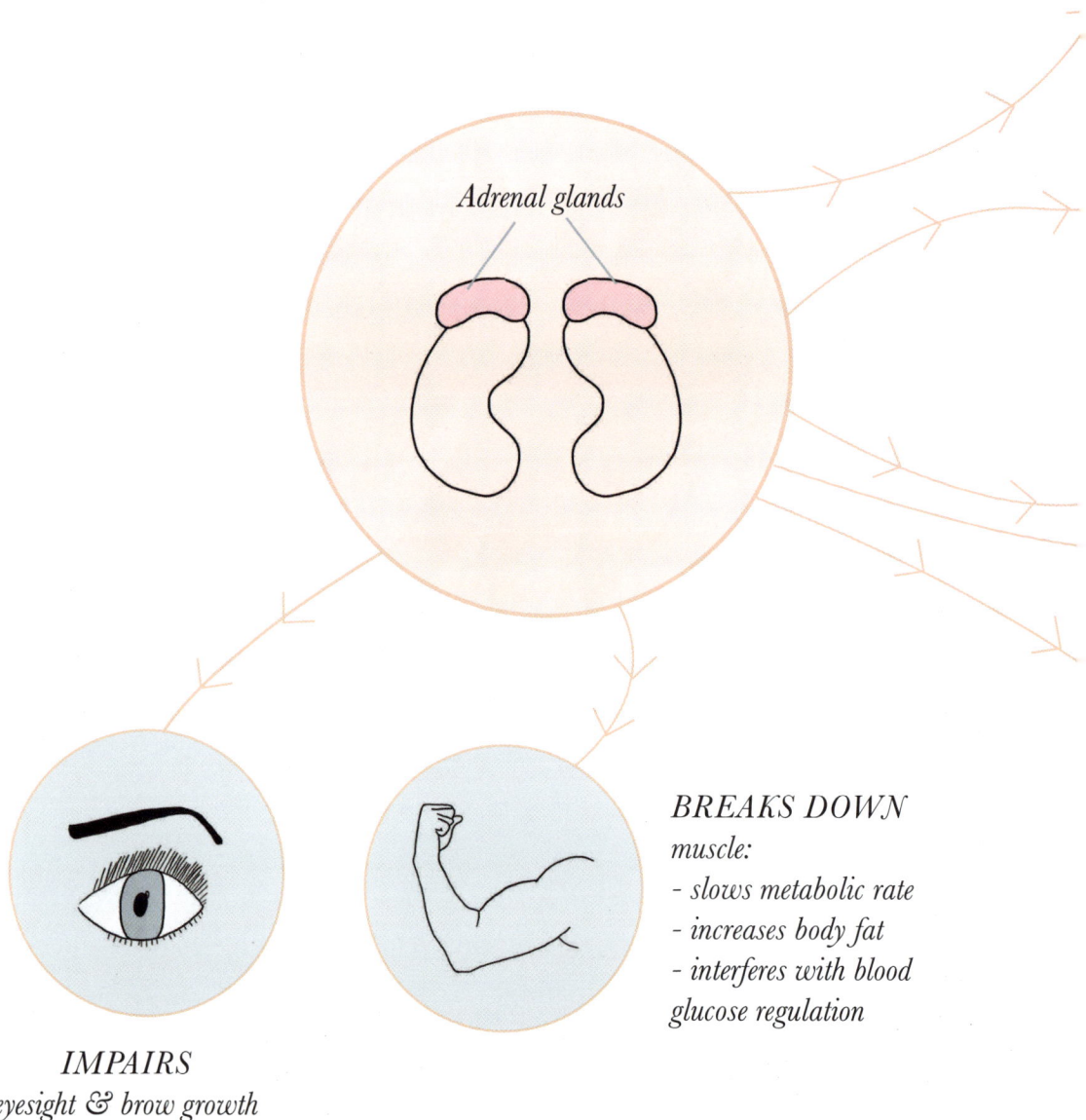

Adrenal glands

IMPAIRS
eyesight & brow growth

BREAKS DOWN
muscle:
- slows metabolic rate
- increases body fat
- interferes with blood
glucose regulation

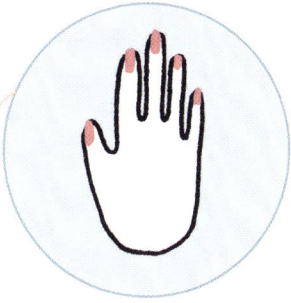

STOPS
hair, skin, nails being
their best

INCREASES
heart rate

INCREASES
blood pressure

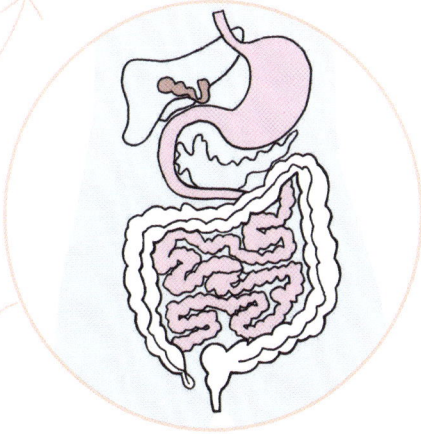

INTERFERES WITH
digestion:
- poor nourishment
- bloating
- IBS-type symptoms

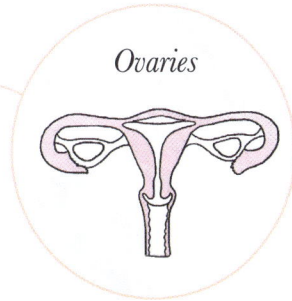

Ovaries

DISRUPTS
sex hormone balance; e.g.
low progesterone:
- decreased fertility
- increased anxious feelings
- increased low mood
- fluid retention

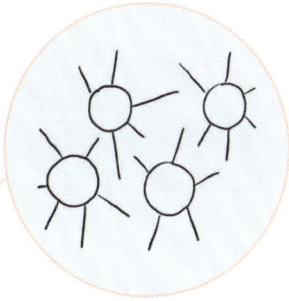

DISRUPTS
immune system
function

Sex hormone overwhelm

When stress tips the balance

When your sex hormones are out of balance, your body tends to let you know. pre-menstrual syndrome (PMS), period pain, tender breasts, headaches, hot flushes, insomnia, constant heat, low mood, weight gain—to name a few.

The sensitive nature of sex hormones means they can act as a barometer of other processes in the body that might require attention and are a good reflection, not only of our reproductive health, but of overall wellbeing.

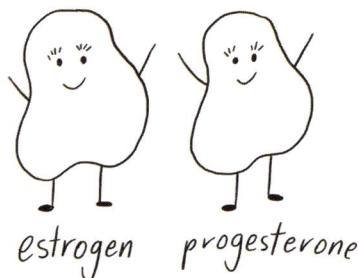

The delicate dance of our sex hormones and stress hormones makes sex hormone imbalances one of the first signs our body will give us when the invisible load of our stress is getting too much. Yet they have become so common these days that many women pass these uncomfortable symptoms off as simply part of being a woman; partly because they feel at a loss about where to start to rebalance them and partly because it almost seems normal for women to suffer with their hormones. The suffering might be common, yet it does not have to be the case.

The relationship between your stress and sex hormones can offer you insight into how you're really coping and how heavy your invisible load might really be. And for those of you who have a regular period, you get a chance each month to tune into what your body thinks about your stress and other lifestyle factors.

Sex Hormones   *Stress Hormones*

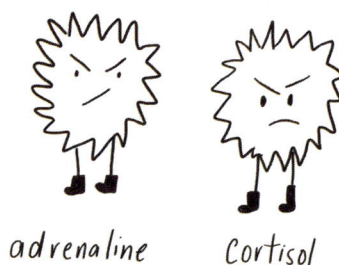

estrogen   progesterone   adrenaline   Cortisol

Before we look at what upsets your sex hormone balance, let's see what an ideal sex hormone picture looks like:

FOR THOSE OF YOU WHO HAVE
A REGULAR PERIOD, YOU GET A
CHANCE EACH MONTH TO TUNE
INTO WHAT YOUR BODY THINKS
ABOUT YOUR STRESS.

A HEALTHY CYCLE

The two main sex hormones for women are estrogen and progesterone; we also make a small amount of testosterone. Two hormones that the pituitary makes are also involved: follicle stimulating hormone (FSH) and luteinising hormone (LH).

From a ratio perspective, in the first half of the cycle estrogen is the dominant sex hormone, laying down the lining of the uterus in preparation for conception. Your body wants you to fall pregnant every month of your reproductive life whether that is something you're considering or not. For the first half of the cycle, you make a small amount of progesterone from your adrenal glands, while the majority will be made after you've ovulated. More on this in a moment. One of progesterone's reproductive jobs is to hold the lining of the uterus in place.

Estrogen lays it down and progesterone has to kick in and hold it there. However, progesterone also plays numerous other biological roles: it is a powerful anti-anxiety agent, an antidepressant and a diuretic, helping us to get rid of excess fluid.

As you've learnt, your adrenal glands are also where you make your stress hormones—adrenaline and cortisol. Remember that adrenaline communicates to every cell in your body that your life is in danger, while cortisol communicates that there is no food. Stress hormone production is always going to be a higher priority for your body than sex hormone production, because your survival is paramount. And because your body links progesterone to fertility, the last thing it wants for you is to bring a baby into a world where it perceives you're not safe and that there's no food!

OUT OF BALANCE, BUT WHY?

I've heard countless people share with me that they feel like their body betrays them. I understand completely why they feel this way, but the truth is your body just responds to the information it is receiving. That statement matters so much. I encourage you to read it again.

PEOPLE FEEL LIKE THEIR BODY BETRAYS THEM, BUT THE TRUTH IS YOUR BODY JUST RESPONDS TO THE INFORMATION IT IS RECEIVING.

So, your body thinks it is doing you a great big favour by shutting down or significantly decreasing your production of progesterone when it is on the receiving end of excessive stress hormone production. This can compromise fertility. Plus, you've now stopped making a hormone that helps you to not feel anxious, helps to stop you going to a low mood, and now you are retaining fluid. For so many women, a distended abdomen and a puffy, swollen feeling leads them into a spiral of supremely hurtful self-talk. And if you don't know that being low in one little hormone can have this effect, you will often start to believe that there must be something wrong with you. When you look out upon your life you can see there is much beauty and so much for which to be grateful (even if there is also tough stuff going on), yet you can't feel it. So, you can unfortunately often add guilt to this cocktail of denigration.

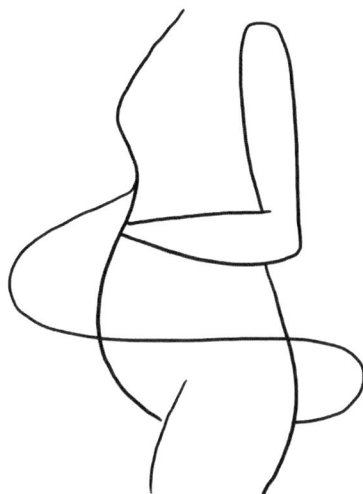

Around mid-cycle, after FSH from the pituitary has helped one of the eggs in one of your ovaries to ripen, a surge of LH drives that ripened egg to be released. A temporary crater remains on the surface of the ovary—called the corpus luteum—and it is from there that you produce a lovely big surge of progesterone. In simpler terms, without ovulation there is no surge in progesterone. Progesterone levels are supposed to peak seven days after you ovulate, so if ovulation occurs on day 14 of your cycle, it will peak on day 21. Usually, seven days after this you start to menstruate (if conception hasn't occurred).

Relatively speaking (not in actual numbers; so much about hormone health comes down to ratios of one hormone to another), your progesterone level is supposed to be higher than your estrogen for the majority of the second half of your cycle, including leading into menstruation. That hormonal picture typically gives you a period that just shows up—how it is supposed to be. No pain, no problems. However, this is not the case for the majority of women I have worked with over the past two decades, and overwhelming stress plays a major role in why.

It's just a few dishes

I can't keep doing this.
EVERYTHING is falling apart!!!

YOUR BODY HAS YOUR BACK

Your body has your best interests at heart and it will only:

1. ovulate if it perceives it is safe for you to do so
2. allow progesterone to surge if it is safe for you to conceive (and even though our conscious mind knows we're 'safe' our bodies are picking up on a different message via the constant and relentless production of stress hormones).

Some women don't ovulate each cycle but still bleed. Others don't ovulate and they don't menstruate. Other women produce progesterone from the corpus luteum, but the hormone doesn't surge. It only peaks above estrogen for a couple of days and then falls away too soon, meaning estrogen is dominant over progesterone in the lead-up to menstruation. This is the hormonal basis of PMS or pre-menstrual tension (PMT) as it is sometimes known, common symptoms of which include swollen, tender breasts, heavy, clotty, painful periods and mood swings that range from immense irritability to intense sadness.

It's also worth mentioning that in my clinical work I have noticed it is very important to pay attention to what bothers you when you have PMT. The situation/s may or may not be real (you might be perceiving or imagining something), but whatever it is, or whatever the THEME is, it is helpful to notice. Because whatever it is likely bothers you all month; it's just that you keep a lid on it for the rest of the month.

Sex hormones across the menstruation years are designed to help us nurture those around us so when these hormones are out of balance, which often typically occurs as menstruation approaches, your inhibitions have left the building. Out pours what bothers you: you don't get enough help around the home or you don't feel loved or appreciated despite all you do are two common ones. There are a million more. So just notice. And see if you can have a conversation about this earlier in the month as your PMT often shows you a need that you can't otherwise identify or express.

Back to the hormones. There are two main hormonal pictures that can create this scenario of estrogen dominance in the second half of the cycle, at which point progesterone is supposed to be dominant. Too much estrogen is one and low progesterone is the other, although these can also occur simultaneously. An overwhelmed liver directly relates to the former, while stress typically relates to the latter.

STRESS AND SAFETY

Previously (page 46), we discussed the way the hypothalamus asks the question 'am I safe?' It has its own response (it makes certain hormones) to whatever the answer is, and it also passes on the information to the pituitary gland. She too responds based on whether the information passed to her indicates you are safe or not—and for many people safety often means feeling loved, appreciated, liked, accepted, or being seen as 'perfect.'
So many people have a constant background (or foreground) noise of fear. Fear of everything: fat, food, letting people down, what others think of them, living in pursuit of perfection as the mask of fear that they (usually unknowingly) wear.

It is not up to the ovary whether she ovulates or not. The pituitary decides this and only sends her hormones to foster this if she has received information that this is the best thing for you. This is one way that stress can lead to low progesterone levels, remembering that if you don't ovulate, you rely completely on your adrenals for the production of this hormone.

But your adrenals too can play a role in compromised progesterone levels as, when they are constantly and relentlessly churning out stress hormones, they do not receive the message that it is safe or appropriate for them to also produce progesterone. So, thinking they are doing you a favour by putting all their resources into saving your life through stress hormone production, they shut down adrenal progesterone production.

Working out what is really behind your stress and the impact of your invisible load is not only important to lower stress hormones themselves and to reduce the consequences they bring, but also because of their ripple effect. And as you can now see, one of those ripples drives compromised sex hormone balance which has truly significant consequences that add to your sense of overwhelm.

LOW PROGESTERONE–
likely due to the
overproduction of
stress hormones.

TOO MUCH
ESTROGEN–
likely due to an
overwhelmed liver.

The load on your liver

Why your sex hormones may be out of balance

The liver also plays a role in whether the sex hormones are balanced or not. While stress hormone overwhelm can all too easily lead to progesterone levels being low, the liver's role in sex hormone metabolism is an essential one to understand. It matters immensely as when this is compromised it can add an exponential load to how you feel each day, and hence your overall invisible load.

When estrogen is dominant over progesterone leading into the menstrual period, it can be due to low progesterone on its own, or high estrogen on its own, or both. And the liver must be addressed in the latter two scenarios, when estrogen is involved.

THE LIVER ITSELF

Before we explore the relationship between estrogen and the liver, let's first understand some vital work the liver does. This extraordinary organ plays many roles in the body, one of which is detoxification, transforming potentially problematic substances so that they don't accumulate in your blood. Put simply, the liver receives substances that, if they were to build up in your blood, might harm you, and it changes them into a less harmful version so you can incorporate them into your urine and/or faeces and eliminate them from your body. The liver loves to decrease your invisible load.

There are technically three stages to detoxification, but we'll just focus on two here as this will assist you in understanding the role the liver plays in helping to regulate estrogen levels. Potentially problematic substances that the liver has to deal with include alcohol, synthetic substances such as pesticides and medications, as well as substances the body makes itself, like cholesterol and estrogen. For this explanation, we'll stay focused on estrogen.

One of the main requirements of the detoxification process is to make the potentially problematic substances more water soluble, as many of them are fat soluble, including estrogen.

This requires a two-step change process referred to as Phase 1 (where substances are transformed initially) and Phase 2 detoxification (where substances are changed again). In other words, the liver has to alter estrogen before it can be eliminated. But this isn't always an efficient process and here's why.

The liver will always prioritise substances you consume before it will deal with what your own body has created, as the body perceives that the risks of damage to your health are far greater from what you've allowed to enter via what you eat, drink, inhale and put on your skin. So when you consider your daily intake of artificial and synthetics substances—sweeteners, colours, flavours, preservatives—as well as alcohol, too many sugars, plus what you wash dishes with, clean your house with and rub into your skin, you can end up with a liver that eventually struggles to keep up with the load. This means that instead of whatever requires detoxification—for our example this is estrogen—undergoing both Phase 1 and Phase 2 detoxification, Phase 1 occurs in a straightforward way, but the Phase 2 pathways have a traffic jam! So if the partially detoxified substance that comes out of Phase 1 cannot enter the next stage of its journey in Phase 2, the best way to picture what happens is that the liver has a trapdoor and it releases this partially detoxified estrogen back out into the blood supply. Remember your body sent the estrogen to the liver as it deemed it best for you that the levels reduce. But now it is back in your blood—in what is considered to be a more reactive and problematic form than what arrived. Talk about adding some rocks to your pack!

When the liver cannot detoxify estrogen efficiently enough, levels of estrogen, relative to progesterone, can become too high. Plus, now you not only have estrogen levels that are too high, but you also have a version of estrogen in that mix that is most undesirable. Gut bacteria also play a role in whether this occurs or not. More on this in a moment.

The greatest fear in the world is the opinions of others. And the moment you are unafraid of the crowd you are no longer a sheep, you become a lion. A great roar arises in your heart, the roar of freedom.

– Osho

PRIORITIES

To reiterate, the liver will always prioritise what it deals with.
And this priority list is based on YOUR SURVIVAL. 'Consumed' before 'home-made', to put it simply. Recycling alcohol is not an option, for example, as if blood levels go too high we go into a coma and can die. Estrogen won't do that.

It can increase our risk of reproductive cancers, but its impacts are not as rapid, or initially, as sinister, as alcohol. So gradually, what tends to happen is that estrogen dominance gets worse and worse.

Although, in saying that, I have worked with hundreds of teenagers over the years suffering terribly with PMT, severe period pain, very heavy bleeding—all symptoms of excessive estrogen—so these challenges with estrogen are starting at younger and younger ages. Environmental estrogen is contributing significantly to this and in some cases to very high body fat levels.

WHERE DOES ESTROGEN COME FROM?

Across the menstruation years, you make estrogen predominantly from your:

- ovaries
- adrenals
- body fat.

Post-menopausally, you predominantly make estrogen from your:

- adrenals
- body fat.

Across our whole lifespan, we ingest and absorb estrogen from the environment as well as synthetic substances that mimic estrogen.

These substances, once inside us, can bind to estrogen receptors. From an evolutionary perspective, this is very new to us as humans and given that girls as young as eight are now menstruating, the consequences are deeply, deeply concerning.

Therefore, across our entire lifetime, it is **essential** that we can efficiently detoxify and eliminate estrogen. Our liver plays a major role in this. If the liver is overwhelmed and focused on dealing with an overconsumption of lousy-quality foods and drinks, estrogen dominance—too much estrogen compared to progesterone leading into the period—is highly likely. Remember that the symptoms of estrogen dominance add to feelings of being overwhelmed and you can usually add irritability and angry, snappy outbursts to the list of symptoms you might experience.

THE ESTROBOLOME

The liver works hand-in-hand with the gut, and part of this interplay involves our gut bacteria. The 'gut microbiome' is a collective term used to describe the bacterial species that inhabit our gut. The 'estrobolome' is the name given to the species of the microbiome that can influence how much estrogen is eliminated in our faecal matter and how much is recycled into the body.

Some bacterial species are capable of producing an enzyme called beta-glucuronidase, which essentially reverses the work that the liver has done to get the estrogen ready for elimination. If you have large populations of these bacteria, you are more likely to end up reabsorbing estrogen, rather than eliminating it efficiently.

Diets high in plant-based foods have been shown to lead to low population levels of beta-glucuronidase-producing bacterial species, [1] yet another reason to be highly focused on ensuring you eat plenty of vegetables. Also seek to minimise (or avoid) your exposure to anything that disrupts the microbiome in the first place. Antibiotics, sulphur-based preservatives in processed food, dried fruits and wine, and artificial sweeteners are all prime suspects.

EXCESS ESTROGEN SYMPTOMS

When there is too much estrogen compared to progesterone leading into the period, common symptoms include:

- recurring headaches or migraines before or during menstruation

- breast swelling and tenderness

- bloating

- nausea, vomiting

- depressed mood

- leg cramps

- yellow tinge to the skin

- excessive vaginal bleeding

- clots in the menstrual blood.

These can all be signs that your estrogen is too high. Obviously, how you eat and drink plays a significant role in the healthy functioning of your gut and liver—both what you include and what you minimise or avoid. Focusing on taking better care of your liver can start to reduce your invisible load and the feeling of being overwhelmed you experience as a result of a sex hormone imbalance driven by too much estrogen.

The ebbs and flows of your life stages

Transitioning through womanhood

We've explored the way overwhelm—specifically via stress and the liver—influences whether sex hormones are balanced or imbalanced during the menstruation years, as well as the roles of estrogen and progesterone. So let's continue across the life stages to examine the way hormonal ebbs and flows are affected by the load we carry.

And, also, what occurs to our sense of overwhelm as our sex hormone levels change. A smooth transition from regular menstruation, through perimenopause to being post-menopausal, is ultimately what we are seeking. Challenging symptoms offer us insight into areas that need support and the changes our body is prompting us to make to how we eat, drink, move, think, breathe and/or perceive.

PERIMENOPAUSE

Perimenopause occurs over a varied amount of time for women, but it is the transition from having monthly, regular periods to them being erratic. You might initially skip two months and then bleed again for three, before missing one, bleeding again, and then not menstruate for five months. Back the period comes, just once this time, before disappearing again for a few more months, perhaps returning again just once (or any version of an irregular pattern).

Then eventually 12 months pass, across which time you don't menstruate. Menopause has occurred when you have not menstruated for 12 months. Then you are post-menopausal.

Across the perimenopausal months or years, or even a decade for some women, with the ebb and flow of menstrual blood comes many changes in sex hormone levels and hence what you experience and feel. During the months in which you don't ovulate, you rely completely on your adrenals for your progesterone. However, as we discussed on page 78, if you are churning out stress hormones, you are unlikely to produce any progesterone from your adrenals and any you might make will likely be converted into cortisol, not kept as progesterone.

This leads you to have a heightening of anxious feelings, a tendency to a low mood and increased fluid retention—all experiences that can create an overwhelmed state, or that can add to an already overwhelmed one. The invisible load becomes far heavier when this is our biochemical picture.

Across the perimenopause years, estrogen levels surge or plummet. When this happens, you tend to overheat, feel easily irritated and engulfed by the intensity of what your body is going through— it might feel like you can't control anything. This also usually contributes to our sense of feeling overwhelmed.

Add to all of this the stress hormones you'll likely have been churning out relentlessly for years (if not decades), plus the SNS dominance that has run your life for too long, and you have a cocktail of hormones tied up in creating this feeling of chaos in your body, the way you react and respond to things, and what you consequently see play out in your life.

When you consider also that body fat levels will likely be increasing if this is the hormonal picture unfolding, there's yet another recipe for overwhelm.

If your food and movement patterns have not changed, key contributors to this are likely to be:

- **Cortisol:** the chronic stress hormone that breaks down muscle and slows metabolic rate.

- **Insulin:** a hormone that regulates blood glucose levels and also drives fat storage when made in excess, which can occur due to the consumption of too many processed foods and/or drinks high in refined carbohydrates, too much caffeine as this elevates blood glucose, adrenaline as this too elevates blood glucose, and being too sedentary.

- **Decreased thyroid hormone production:** explained in an upcoming section; you'll be fascinated at how stress affects thyroid function.

- **Fatty liver:** interferes with efficient detoxification of everything so more rubbish gets stored away in your body fat, increasing your total body burden.

- **SNS dominance (from real or perceived stress, worry and tension):** pushing primarily glucose to be used as a fuel rather than fat.

- **Altered/unfavourable gut bacteria profiles:** due to poor diet quality and antibiotic use in the past, this can influence how much calories are worth and can drive metabolic changes.

And with decreasing estrogen levels the closer you get to menopause comes another addition to the body fat increase list.

MENOPAUSE

When you have not had a period for more than 12 months, by definition, you are post-menopausal. By this time, some or all of the symptoms of perimenopause described previously have abated for some women—but not all. When there is ongoing heat, a common and debilitating problem for many, your first port of call needs to be increasing your care for your liver and altering your lifestyle choices that impact this.

If there is ongoing sleeplessness, let's get to the bottom of that. Is it due to heat? Focus on the liver. Is it due to a wired-type of feeling or worry? Focus on activating the PNS to get out of SNS dominance and lowering adrenaline via diaphragmatic breathing.

Remember that, because adrenaline communicates to every cell in your body that your life is in danger, it is a common interferer in good-quality sleep. Your body thinks that if it lets you sleep deeply and restoratively when you have high circulating levels of adrenaline, you risk not being able to save your own life and flee! Yet another example of how your body has your back.

Have body fat levels continued to the rise in estrogen through your transition into menopause, despite your efforts? On top of the reasons listed in the perimenopause section, stress and overwhelm can create yet another driver of this.

When estrogen levels fall low due to the ceasing of the ovarian production of hormones, your adrenal glands can produce estrogen to ease you into your new lower-level norm of this hormone. But if you've been overwhelmed and your long-term output of stress hormones has been constant and relentless, you may not have made sex hormones from your adrenal glands for years or decades. So, when your ovaries stop their production of estrogen, the adrenals don't suddenly jump back into action with sex hormone production, as they are likely still churning out stress hormones, with the hypothalamus and pituitary screaming that you're not safe.

BECAUSE ADRENALINE COMMUNICATES TO EVERY CELL IN YOUR BODY THAT YOUR LIFE IS IN DANGER, IT IS A COMMON INTERFERER IN GOOD-QUALITY SLEEP.

Body fat cells have the capacity to produce estrogen so, in this situation, the body thinks it is doing you a favour by increasing body fat levels in an attempt to give you more estrogen and ease your suffering. So much ill health and aspects of our body that frustrate or sadden us boil down to the body responding to the information it is receiving. And when that information has been filled with stress hormones for such a long time, the impact of being overwhelmed across our life stages has to be addressed, not only for the benefit of this generation of women going through menopause but for future generations too.

We must ensure women of all ages and stages have the skills to get to the heart of what is really driving their stress so they can turn off the tap and only produce stress hormones when they really need them. Health and life quality need us to spend far less time with the stress response activated.

Any steps we can take towards decreasing how often stress hormones are elevated is going to help sex hormones regain and maintain balance, whether we are menstruating, perimenopausal or post-menopausal. This will inevitably lead to reducing the sense of everyday overwhelm that too many women unnecessarily experience.

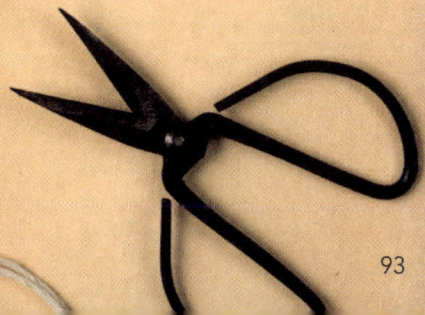

Hormonal swings

How sex hormones can add to the load

We tend to think that our worries drive our stress—everything out there—but does the changing landscape of our sex hormones alter how we deal with and respond to our worries, as well as what we actually worry about? Essentially, do we 'cope' better, shift our focus more easily, no matter what's on our plates, when our sex hormones are balanced? I offer up a resounding YES! As a result, it is an area where you can quite powerfully help yourself and remove some rocks from your pack.

Until people have a deeper understanding of their body and the wide variety of roles sex hormones play, I have found they enormously underestimate the significant role an imbalance of sex hormones plays in the thoughts that arise and the way they think. This includes their ability to overcome a downward spiral of judgement—of others or themselves—or debilitatingly harsh self-talk, a constant tirade of put-downs.

Or perhaps it shows up for you more like this. You are part of a group of friends and you like them all. For the most part, you are fine with the group dynamic and you don't even think about (let alone are bothered by) the fact that two girls in the group are now closer to each other than they are with you, when a year ago that wasn't the case and you were closer with one of them. Most of the time, you don't even think about their closeness and if you do, your heart is genuinely happy for their deepened kinship.

Then, in what feels like out of nowhere, green-eyed thoughts, which you can't even initially name as jealousy, ferociously rear their head and you are so distracted from your work and study that you can't progress anything for chunks of time while your brain seemingly latches onto the friendship they have that feels so separate from you. And then hours or days later, whoosh, that churned-up feeling has exited stage right and you are back to your status quo. And you shake your head at yourself wondering what on earth just happened.

How can you feel peaceful, or certainly not at all bothered, one day and almost scorned the next? With no shades of grey, your emotional landscape scoots from one pole to another.

You might know better. Or not. Yet you might notice that there are times when these thoughts take over your existence and you can't seem to scramble your way to the surface of how you felt perhaps only last week or even an hour ago.

Of course, aspects of our psychology and beliefs play a major role in this, but that's a topic for another page. I want this to help you become a thought detective, your own inspiring, deeply caring thought leader, so you can truly decipher and understand if your hormones are contributing to your stress and adding to your load in a moment-to-moment or day-to-day way. So, start to pay attention to when these kinds of thoughts arise and consider where you might be in your menstrual cycle to see if there's a pattern.

ANOTHER ANGLE

In the previous scenario you do know the truth deep down. That is, you are happy your friends have each other. Then there are other situations where you know deep down that something is not acceptable to you, yet you don't communicate it. When patients would share with me their tales and, at times, traumas of PMS or tricky perimenopausal months, I would always encourage them not to dismiss what had bubbled to the surface.

For hormonally, as the period approaches, and if our hormones are not balanced at this time, it tends to show you what is really bothering you. It's just that for the rest of the month, you block it out, justify the behaviour of another and your nurturing, 'tend and befriend' hormones help you to 'keep the peace'. Yet in the lead-up to your period, you feel anything but peaceful.

AS THE PERIOD APPROACHES, AND IF OUR HORMONES ARE NOT BALANCED AT THIS TIME, IT TENDS TO SHOW YOU WHAT IS REALLY BOTHERING YOU.

When there is not enough progesterone (on its own or coupled with too much estrogen) it is possible that you may find it very difficult to not go to overwhelm, as the level of one of the key hormones that stops you going there is through the floor.

The key here is to know which scenario it is, and your heart always knows. Is it the situation where your hormones rile you up into a frenzied worry about being left out of a friendship? Do your hormones make you dream up concepts like 'being left out'? And when you pause to consider this, you are truly not bothered at all —it is that ancient fear of not being loved that has simply been triggered and yet your adult self knows better. Or is it situation two, where your hormones **show you** what is there all month? And when you pause to examine it, you want more help around the house all month, not just when you voice it near your period.

This might be a dynamic in the home that needs to change. Another common scenario could be that you're a 'yes' person and yet when your period comes around, you just want to shut the door on everyone and everything. This is your body suggesting that you start flexing your 'no' muscle more frequently, not just in the lead-up to your period. Plus, it is natural to need more quiet time and rest just before and across the first few days of menstruation.

I believe we all need to be more responsible for our words, behaviours and thoughts. Do your best to be more attentive to your thoughts and if you see that sex hormones might be influencing them, don't just brush them aside. Notice what's there. Is this a made-up story or something you have identified is important to you? Are you responding to what is really happening in your life, or a story you've made up about what is occurring?

Do your best to halt thought trains that want to run away with imaginings of possibilities that if they were to occur would stress you out. Catch the thoughts and tell yourself to stop the imaginings and come back to deal with what is right here. For so much that we conjure up and worry about never eventuates, and you just unnecessarily hurt yourself in the process.

1× SAY NO
VOUCHER
UNLIMITED USES • GUILT FREE

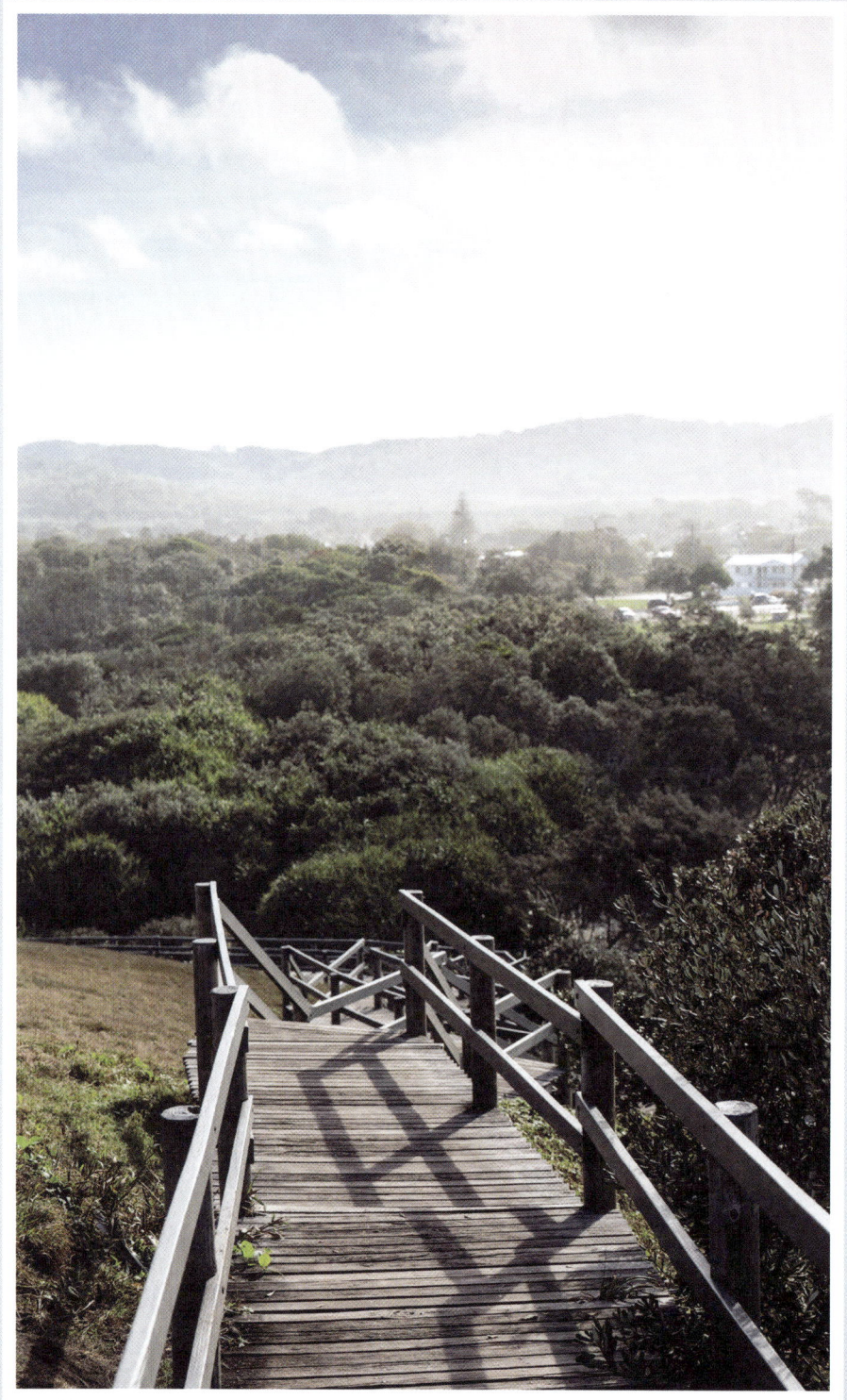

To recap

Out-of-balance sex hormones, which are almost always a result of the constant and relentless output of stress hormones, can lead you to a way of thinking, not to mention eating, sleeping and reacting, that hurts you.

You want to discern the 'what is' and deal with that. Don't allow yourself to get caught up in imaginings. Even just doing this alone makes an enormous difference to your emotional health.

Do your absolute, committed best to deal with what is right here in front of you in this moment, not a story your mind is making up.

It can help to ask your heart, 'does this really matter?' and act on your response—no matter whether it is challenging, uncomfortable or difficult. Ultimately, doing this will lead you to be more aligned with your values, which will decrease your sense of being overwhelmed and flood you with relief.

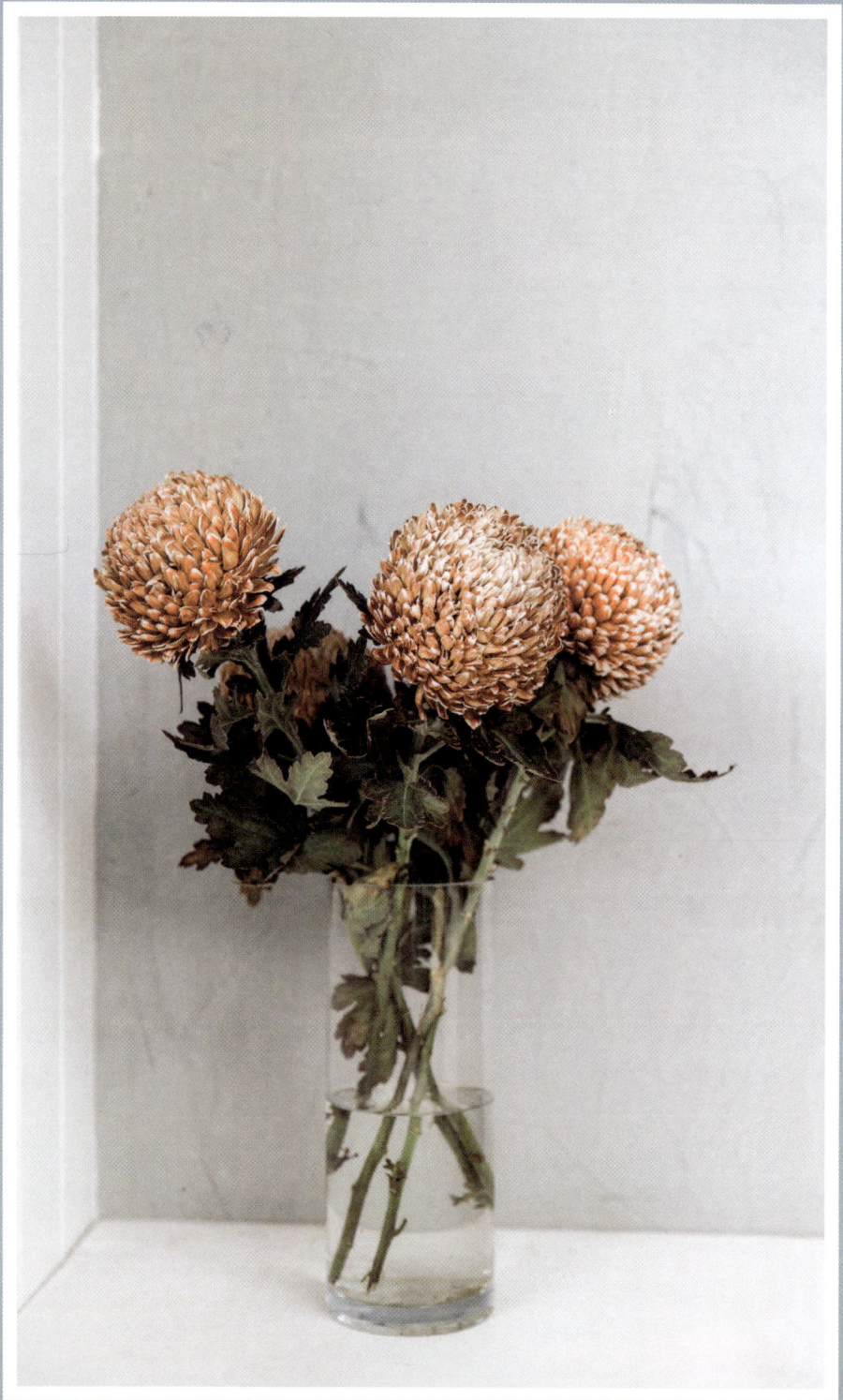

Is it my thyroid?

When it feels like something isn't quite right

The thyroid gland often arises as a concern for women when they feel like something is not quite right in their body. Whether there have been increasing levels of fatigue, clothes are getting tighter for inexplicable reasons, or they have begun to feel less optimistic about life in general—a downturn in mood—questions about the optimal function of the thyroid are wise to be raised as this can add an enormous weight to your invisible load.

Many women have read that they need good thyroid function to have a decent metabolic rate and when they google the symptoms of an underactive thyroid, they feel like they tick a number of the boxes (see the list of symptoms on page 112). Yet when they see their GP to have it tested, they are told it is normal. Before we dig in and examine how it is possible that you have a certain set of symptoms yet 'normal' test results, let's understand how the thyroid works, how it receives and produces information and how that translates into how you feel.

As with other communication pathways in the endocrine system, this one too begins with the hypothalamus producing a hormone to send to the pituitary. In the case of thyroid regulation, it is thyrotropin-releasing hormone (TRH), which signals to the pituitary that it needs to produce thyroid stimulating hormone (TSH).

TSH is the wake-up call to the thyroid gland itself to make its hormones: thyroxine (T4) and triiodothyronine (T3). The former is inactive and has to be converted into the latter, which drives all of the metabolic functions for which the thyroid is responsible. Thyroid hormones work on every cell in the body so when the gland doesn't work efficiently, the symptoms are often multi-factorial.

For this cascade of hormones to flow, and for the right amount of each hormone to be produced, specific nutrients are required—iodine, selenium and iron in particular—as is a healthy balance between estrogen and progesterone.

THE NUTRIENTS

The key nutrients for good thyroid function and hormone production include iodine, selenium and iron. The structures of T4 and T3 are so reliant on iodine because the numbers in their names actually represent the number of iodine units that need to be attached to the foundation structure for the hormone to be produced. Selenium is also needed for thyroid hormone synthesis, activation and metabolism. In fact, the human thyroid gland is supposed to have the highest selenium content per gram of tissue, of all the organs in the body. [1]

Iron is somewhat different again in the role it plays in thyroid hormone production. T4, being the inactive thyroid hormone, has to be converted into T3, the active thyroid hormone, to do its metabolism-driving work. However, in an iron-deficient state, instead of T4 being efficiently converted into T3, some of the T4 gets converted into a different hormone called reverseT3 (rT3), which does not have the same metabolism-promoting effects of T3. Additionally, rT3 can block the effects of T3. Too much rT3 is also thought to be produced during chronic stress, again yet another mechanism that interferes with the body's ability to use body fat efficiently as a fuel.

Although more research is needed, too much rT3 is thought have an additional flow-on effect: it makes the body go deaf to leptin, a hormone responsible for letting you know when you've had enough to eat. Leptin is made by fat cells as a way of regulating appetite and how much body fat is retained. It is thought that the rT3 interferes with your ability to hear leptin's messages. So! Good thyroid hormone production is essential to us feeling good via multiple mechanisms.

EXCESS ESTROGEN

Yet another substance that can interfere with good thyroid function, and one that is all too common today, is long-term excessive amounts of estrogen. Excess estrogen suppresses thyroid function while the right amount of progesterone supports thyroid function. Too much or too little of any hormone has consequences.

It is just that, these days, many women are estrogen dominant—there is too much estrogen and not enough progesterone—and if this goes on for too long, poor thyroid function can be a potential outcome.

THE ROAD IN IS
THE ROAD OUT

Whatever it is that created the thyroid problem in the first place needs to be understood, as the road in is the road that needs to be taken out of the problem. For example, if it was iodine deficiency that led the thyroid to not work efficiently, increasing dietary iodine will likely correct this. But if the thyroid is not working properly due to long-term estrogen dominance, no amount of iodine will resolve the thyroid dysfunction. Addressing the estrogen dominance will.

ALL CELLS IN THE BODY RESPOND TO INCREASES IN THYROID HORMONES, INCREASING THE RATE AT WHICH THEY CONDUCT THEIR TASKS.

This is an enormous reason why I am passionate about people knowing HOW things work so they can then make more informed choices.

A COMMON ROAD TO THYROID PROBLEMS
TODAY IS THIS:

1. Relentless adrenaline production speeds everything up so thyroid hormone production decreases in an attempt to compensate.

2. Poor dietary intake of the nutrients needed for good thyroid hormone production occurs: low intake of iodine, selenium and iron; you might become iron deficient which increases rT3 production and blocks T3 activity as well as leptin's messages being heard so your body wants to store fat.

3. You might be iron deficient from poor dietary intake or excessive menstrual blood loss. If it is the latter, this can be a sign of estrogen excess, as is PMT. Excess estrogen interferes with thyroid hormone production further.

BLOOD TESTS

Now back to those blood tests. There is some conjecture about whether blood tests for thyroid hormones give us the full picture of thyroid health. For now, that's all we have so we need to work with it. When I was seeing patients, I would always couple blood test results with the symptoms the patient was exhibiting, under the proviso that the body doesn't lie. I always treated the body, the individual and used the blood test results as a guide. And here's why.

Firstly, I am concerned about how 'normal' ranges are established in the first place, but that is not a conversation for this book (I wrote about it in *Accidentally Overweight*). In New Zealand and Australian pathology laboratories, the 'normal' range for TSH is 0.4 to 4. Do you think someone with a TSH of 0.4 feels or looks anything like someone with a TSH of 4? Unlikely. Yet we need normal ranges, otherwise it would be chaos.

The normal range of T4 Down Under is usually about 10 to 20. A common picture I've seen is not a thyroid disease but rather what I refer to as thyroid dysfunction, and it shows up for the person with symptoms of an underactive thyroid. Their blood work will often present as something like this:

TSH: 3 (0.4–4)	T4: 11 (10–20)

Let's say this person is 48 years old when this is found. She won't get a call-back because her levels are in the normal range. Yet if she'd had blood tests done when she was at her best level of health—let's say when she was 26 years old—her blood work might have looked like this:

TSH: 1 (0.4–4)	T4: 15 (10–20)

In other words, at age 48, the pituitary is having to make three times what is ideal for this individual to try to wake up the thyroid gland to make its hormones, and all it can muster with all this attempted stimulation by the pituitary is 11 measly units of T4.

An overactive thyroid will typically be outside of the normal ranges in the opposite direction to this example.

Or it may just be skewed towards being overactive. That might look like this:

TSH: 0.5 (0.4–4)	T4: 18 (10–20)

The T3 for this person will usually be elevated or elevated within the normal range, too.

In my experience, if you catch a thyroid that is skewed one way and work out what has led the body to think that this is the right response for you, you can treat the cause, rather than provide a band-aid. It's important to consider:

- Is it stress-related?
- Is it a nutrient/s deficiency?
- It is long-term estrogen excess?

Two other factors can also affect the thyroid: infection and what I refer to as liver congestion, poor detoxification and therefore inefficient clearance of problematic substances. Even more so when there is dysbiosis in the gut.

It is known that infective organisms—viruses, bacteria, parasites—can take up residence inside us, and sometimes in organs. If this happens, the body mounts an immune response against it, with view to the foreign organism dying and exiting the body.

However, there is some suggestion now that ongoing autoimmune thyroid diseases indicate that there might be a chronic, low-grade infection still occurring which is why antibody levels keep increasing. Antibodies are substances measurable in blood that show up when the immune system is attacking one of your own tissues, rather than a germ.

In New Zealand and Australia, the two main thyroid auto-antibodies that are tested are anti-thyroglobulin and anti-thyroid peroxidase. They are both supposed to be less than 60 units in New Zealand and Australian pathology laboratories, and they can be worth having tested if you have symptoms of an underactive thyroid but it isn't definitive from your blood test results.

And if they are negative, yet you know your body and your symptoms are clear to you, you might like to consider chronic stress as the driver of the thyroid not working as well as it could. It is rife, after all. Let's dig deeper into that now.

Deal with what is,
not imaginings.

DR LIBBY

Thyroid dysfunction

Signs to look out for

When it comes to an overwhelmed thyroid gland, it is important to know that the thyroid has numerous levels of dysfunction. There are thyroid diseases, such as Hashimoto's thyroiditis and Graves' disease, and there are also thyroid glands that aren't at the point of disease diagnosis but rather they just don't work well.

A thyroid disease will show up distinctively in your blood test results, with values falling outside the 'normal' reference ranges. Thyroid dysfunction usually won't, although results are often skewed to one end of the 'normal range'.

With the latter, you typically experience some of the symptoms of one of the thyroid diseases, but when your test results come back in the 'normal range' you'll be told that there is nothing wrong with your thyroid. Yet, you continue to suspect otherwise.

AN UNDERACTIVE THYROID IS CALLED HYPOTHYROIDISM. AN OVERACTIVE THYROID IS CALLED HYPERTHYROIDISM.

Before we go into how stress and your invisible load can interfere with thyroid function, let's explore some of the signs your body gives you that your thyroid isn't working optimally, whether the relentless output of stress hormones is behind them or there are some other driving factor/s.

An underactive thyroid is called hypothyroidism (remember 'o' for 'low'). An overactive thyroid is called hyperthyroidism. Autoimmune responses—where the immune system mounts an immune response against one of your own tissues instead of a foreign substance like a germ—can also affect the thyroid gland, and when this occurs there will be antibodies present in the blood.

When the thyroid is underactive and there are antibodies present it is called Hashimoto's thyroiditis, while hyperthyroidism with the presence of antibodies is called Graves' disease.

Whether antibodies are present or not, some of the symptoms of a **thyroid that is on the underactive** spectrum include:

- menstrual cycle problems that might range from irregular periods, a long cycle (35 days plus), blood loss might be heavy or very light (factors other than just thyroid function impact this, which is why there is not one, clear-cut menstrual cycle challenge style)

- you feel cold easily; feel cold in your bones and find it difficult to warm up

- gradual weight gain, for no obvious reason

- fatigued, not just tired

- tendency to a depressed mood, forgetfulness and a sense of being easily confused

- hair loss or your hair is consistently drier than it was previously

- tendency to constipation

- hoarse voice that is often more noticeable when you are particularly tired

- difficulty conceiving.

When the **thyroid is overactive**, the symptoms typically include:

- easily overheating or heat intolerance (remember this can also indicate that the liver needs some support and/or estrogen levels are fluctuating, which often occurs during perimenopause)

- weight loss for no other reason, although this doesn't always occur as there is sometimes a concomitant increase in appetite and people might eat enough to compensate for the increased metabolic rate that an excess of thyroid hormones provides; hence weight loss is not always noted

- racing heart, heart palpitations, fast heart rate

- poor sleep, insomnia

- eyeballs bulging forward from the socket

- feeling breathless easily

- anxious-type feelings, nervousness

- staring gaze

- increased bowel movements, stools may be loose

- menstrual periods that are very light or absent

- hands tremble sometimes

- tired, but more wired than tired

- hair loss.

Thyroid hormones impact all organs, including the heart, which beats faster under the influence of elevated thyroid hormone levels. All cells in the body respond to increases in thyroid hormones, increasing the rate at which they conduct their tasks.

There are numerous consequences to this, one of which is a different type of stress to feeling overwhelmed but is a potent withdrawal from the health bank account: oxidative stress, which occurs when too many molecules have unpaired electrons (like a unit of oxygen who has lost his buddy), so they are highly reactive and can damage your tissues. As an aside, antioxidants—found predominantly in our coloured plant foods—protect us from damage from oxidative stress.

And now for the main event and another reason, on top of nutrient deficiencies and too much estrogen, that we are seeing more and more thyroid problems: how the constant and relentless output of stress hormones leads to the thyroid becoming dysfunctional. If this is not picked up and resolved, it is yet another road to a thyroid disease.

Consider what thyroid hormones are supposed to do. Put simply, they are supposed to maintain the speed of everything—cellular function, for example, and as a result of this, metabolic rate. Hence the involvement of the thyroid in many people's body weight challenges today.

And what does adrenaline initially do? Speed things up. Amps you to fight or flee. What occurs physiologically in response to increased adrenaline levels? Heart rate increases, we feel more anxious and wired, our breathing rate increases, we might need to run to the loo … all symptoms that occur in response to (too many) thyroid hormones.

So, in response to this, the pituitary says to the thyroid, 'we're a bit amped today. She's really feeling the impact of all the rocks in her backpack at the moment. And she can't seem to throttle back on the adrenaline production because she's smashing herself with coffee and a relentless perception of pressure; she really does carry a huge load that no one really helps her out with and so her brain never stops with the task list; plus she worries constantly about letting people down and what they think of her'. So, because the pituitary is not getting the message from her racing heart to make some changes in order to produce less adrenaline, she says, 'we can't add thyroid hormones to this mix, so let's tone back a bit on their production'. If this were to happen, say, four times a year for 48 hours at a time—no problem. But for most, this happens day in and day out. And eventually this new pattern gets set: stress hormone production that is never dealt with and therefore rarely switched off—you just divert your attention every now and again with the stress record playing in the background.

When stress hormone production is constant and relentless, it's not just the thyroid gland itself potentially releasing fewer thyroid hormones due to the messages it is receiving from the pituitary gland. Other factors throughout the body can disrupt good thyroid hormone production. Markers of inflammation in the blood (called cytokines) which are released during the stress response, have been shown to lower TSH, as well as decrease the conversion of inactive T4 into active T3. Add to this the fact that for thyroid hormones to do their job, they have to be taken up by cells and both excess cortisol and certain cytokines interfere with this process. That means the thyroid hormones don't get to where they need to go to be effective so you get the symptoms of having a thyroid problem. When really it is the stress response messing with your body's ability to *utilise* thyroid hormones.

It is not only iron deficiency that drives poor conversion of inactive T4 to active T3 (as we discussed on page 104) by pushing the T4 to be converted into reverse T3 (rT3), but the ongoing stress response also does this. Cortisol, in particular, has been shown to stop good T3 production due to shifting the conversion of T4 to rT3. And it is not just psychological stress that drives elevated cortisol and this disruption to good thyroid hormone levels and activity; other forms of stress your body perceives, such as restrictive dieting, will do this too. No good comes from not eating enough food.

Why not listen to me?

Then you have the autoimmune thyroid conditions and their relationship to stress. I don't think I can recall a case of thyroid-related autoimmunity that didn't have stress as a major contributing factor that had to be addressed. When someone had a thyroid problem, I tended not to treat the thyroid on its own, always addressing the adrenals and often also the liver, gut and immune system to help someone improve their thyroid parameters and how they were feeling. In fact, I regularly wondered if the thyroid only went awry as a secondary consequence of something else not working efficiently.

Stress (psychological and physical, such as infection or inadequate food intake) is considered to be a potential trigger of autoimmune thyroid conditions and it is well established that cortisol suppresses appropriate immune responses. Nothing in the body stands alone.

These are yet further examples of how your body has your back. You get frustrated that your thyroid doesn't seem to be working properly. Yet nothing inside you sets out to hurt you or frustrate you or make you unhappy. The body is always trying to protect you and keep you well, yet it has to respond to the information it receives. If constantly elevated adrenaline or cortisol levels, for example, are at the heart of your thyroid no longer working effectively, let that prompt you to truly explore your stress and what it really is for you.

TO HELP THIS THYROID STORY MAKE SENSE, HERE'S A RECAP ON HOW IT COMES TOGETHER.

The hypothalamus assesses how EVERYTHING is in the body. Is she safe? What's her heart rate? What about her hormone levels? The list is almost endless.

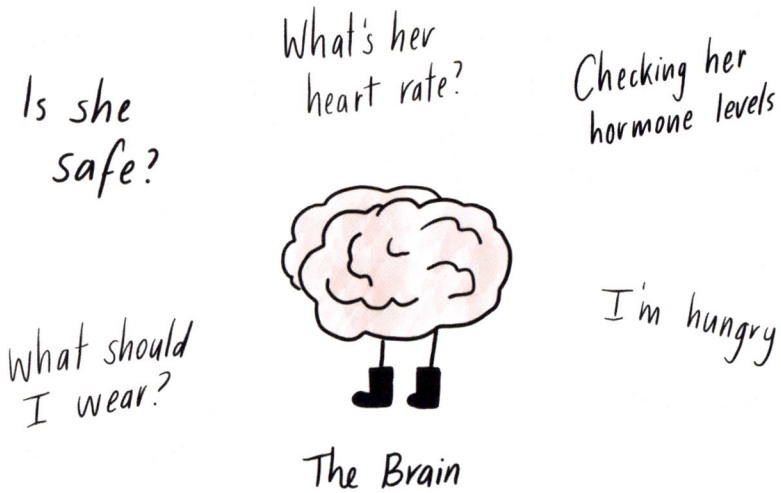

What's her heart rate?

Is she safe?

Checking her hormone levels

what should I wear?

I'm hungry

The Brain

It then makes TRH if it decides that the thyroid needs to produce some of its hormones. Remember that TRH is a message for the pituitary to make her hormone TSH that communicates with the thyroid.

The pituitary makes TSH in the amount deemed appropriate for the thyroid to receive so it can wake up and make the right amount of its hormones, T4 and T3. To do this efficiently you need optimal levels of iodine, selenium, zinc and iron and good sex hormone balance, rather than estrogen dominance.

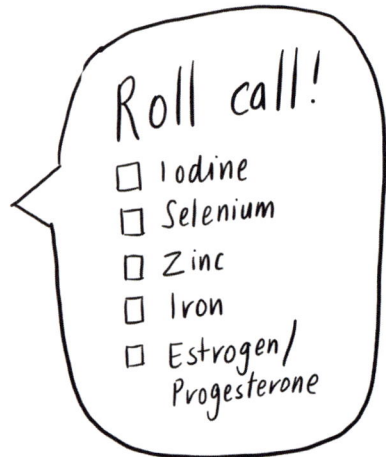

Roll call!
- ☐ Iodine
- ☐ Selenium
- ☐ Zinc
- ☐ Iron
- ☐ Estrogen/ Progesterone

But! Because adrenaline drives a similar state to the one that thyroid hormones create, if you are already wired on adrenaline and under the influence of its effects, the thyroid doesn't think it is in your best interests to keep producing your usual amount of thyroid hormones so its function slows, in an attempt to look after you. This can lead to an underactive thyroid. If adrenaline levels stay elevated and the thyroid doesn't slow down production for other reasons, an overactive scenario can unfold.

ADRENALINE is already here !!!

The Survival Playlist
19'

Cortisol also disrupts thyroid hormone production and the ability of each cell to use it. Both stress hormones affect how much stimulation the thyroid gland receives to make its hormones and how much thyroid hormone is active in the body through various mechanisms. Chronic stress can also be a trigger for autoimmune thyroid conditions. When there are thyroid problems—autoimmune related or otherwise—stress reduction needs to be a top priority.

Gut health

Understanding digestion

The digestive system is another place where the consequences of your invisible load can present—you only have to experience a sore tummy or excessive bloating to know how much this impacts the way you think and your tolerance levels. Before we examine that, though, it's important to understand how aspects of digestion work. We have to know how something works before we can understand what can go wrong.

Picture your digestive system as a tube that begins at the mouth and ends where the waste leaves your body. Everything between the beginning and the end exists so that your Earth Suit can obtain the nutrients you require to stay alive and ideally thrive. This tube also decides what it allows to 'enter' your body, by travelling from the gut across into the blood, so its role is major and central to every other aspect of our health. If this system is not working well, you feel it in myriad places. For example, it can be difficult to have balanced sex hormones when you have increased intestinal permeability, which then changes liver detoxification processes, potentially leading to excess estrogen—you can see how the load can compound. Most health challenges begin with some aspect of gut dysfunction.

When we eat food, we are supposed to chew it well before swallowing, bathing the food that has entered our mouths with their first exposure to digestive enzymes. The job of the teeth is to begin to break the food down, before it continues on its journey of being even further broken down. The action of chewing also stimulates the stomach to release acid which is essential for excellent digestion.

So, down the oesophagus the food goes, at the bottom of which it travels through a valve and lands in the stomach. Your stomach is the size of your own clenched fist when it is empty, but it has the ability to stretch to accommodate your meal. Once food arrives into the stomach it will remain in that little pouch for a period of time (it can take anywhere from 30 minutes to 3 hours for a meal to fully empty out of the stomach) to allow further digestive processes to occur.

Stomach acid—which as the name suggests is a highly acidic substance with a very low pH—and other substances that the cells that line the stomach make, act on the partially broken-down food that arrives. After this, it travels through another valve at the bottom end of the stomach and it enters the small intestine. The pancreas, one of the ancillary organs to the digestive system, releases bicarbonate to raise the pH, and digestive enzymes into the small intestine.

The cells that line this early part of the small intestine also secrete more digestive enzymes. The food continues on its way along the small intestine and, at various points along the tube, nutrients are absorbed out of the food and move across into the blood. This is how you are nourished. This process keeps you alive.

Down low on your abdomen on the right-hand side of your body, you can estimate where the next valve is, through which the very well broken down food, which is getting close to being all waste by now, will continue to travel. If you place your little finger on your right hip bone and stretch your hand out so that your thumb touches your navel, about halfway along that diagonal line you have made with your fingers is another valve where the small intestine becomes the large intestine.

The large intestine contains bacteria that do vital work for your wellbeing. There is some conjecture about how much is actually in the large intestine but it is estimated to be somewhere between half a kilogram and four kilograms.

Bacteria ferment what they are given and produce many important substances essential to health. They also communicate with each other as well as with the brain, and even make substances that people often link to the brain such as certain neurotransmitters like serotonin. We actually now understand that a range of neurotransmitters play a significant role in how the gut works.

Adrenaline, noradrenaline, dopamine, as well as serotonin, affect nutrient absorption, gut motility, the immune system that lines the gut as well as the microbiome. [1] Most of your immune system also lines the digestive system, which makes sense as this is the main way that problematic substances can enter.

THE pH GRADIENT

Every area along the 'tube' of the digestive system has an ideal pH range within which the body tries to maintain. The ideal pH of stomach acid is about 1.9 which is highly acidic—and it needs to be. Stomach acid must be very acidic to do its critical breakdown work on the food you've ideally chewed well before swallowing. Imagine your food starts off as pearls on a string. Your teeth initially loosen the pearls and it is the stomach acid that starts to take them off the string, or break the string itself into sections with, say, 10 pearls per section. When we don't chew our food well, we ask more of our stomach acid and/or other aspects of digestive function may be compromised further down the track.

When the bolus of food leaves the stomach and moves into the first part of the small intestine, the release of bicarbonate by the pancreas into this area swiftly increases the pH. It then gradually rises as the tube continues so that by the time waste leaves the body the pH is almost neutral, otherwise it burns your bottom (which you sometimes see occurring with babies, as their digestive system is immature at birth).

THE IDEAL PH OF STOMACH ACID IS ABOUT 1.9 WHICH IS HIGHLY ACIDIC—AND IT NEEDS TO BE.

THE pH SCALE

0   1   2   3   4   5   6   7   8   9   10   11   12   13   14

Acidic   Neutral   Alkaline

Brilliant
Brassica Soup

The vast variety of gut bacteria species that live in the large intestine each have their own ideal pH range within which they can survive. In the same way the human species can survive on Earth because the temperature range is suitable for our body, as are the atmospheric elements, plus we have access to sources of nitrogen, potassium, phosphorus and all of the other nutrients our structure requires to function. Gut bacteria have certain requirements too and one is an ideal pH range. In other words, if the pH of the area of the gut where they are supposed to live is not suitable for them, they cannot survive. And they won't be able to move back in there until the pH issue is resolved.

For this reason, it is very easy to think that when you have a bloated abdomen that something must have gone awry with your large intestine. Yet where the disruption quite often occurs is earlier on in the process with the stomach acid. For example, if the stomach acid pH is still in the acidic end of the spectrum, but it is at 4 instead of 1.9, it doesn't have the intensity to do its critical breakdown work effectively. This means that poorly broken-down food moves further on into the digestive system than is ideal. It also means that the pH changes the whole way along the digestive tract, making it, in places, inhospitable to the bacterial species you need to be living in there for great health in general as well as digestion. Nothing can live in conditions that aren't suitable to its needs.

> WHEN YOU HAVE A BLOATED STOMACH AND YOU THINK YOU JUST NEED SOME PROBIOTICS, REMEMBER THAT THE PROBLEM MAY HAVE STARTED HIGHER UP

SUPPORTING GOOD STOMACH ACID PRODUCTION AND AN IDEAL pH GRADIENT

So, when you have a bloated stomach and you think you just need some probiotics, remember that the problem may have started higher up the digestive system with poor stomach acid production.

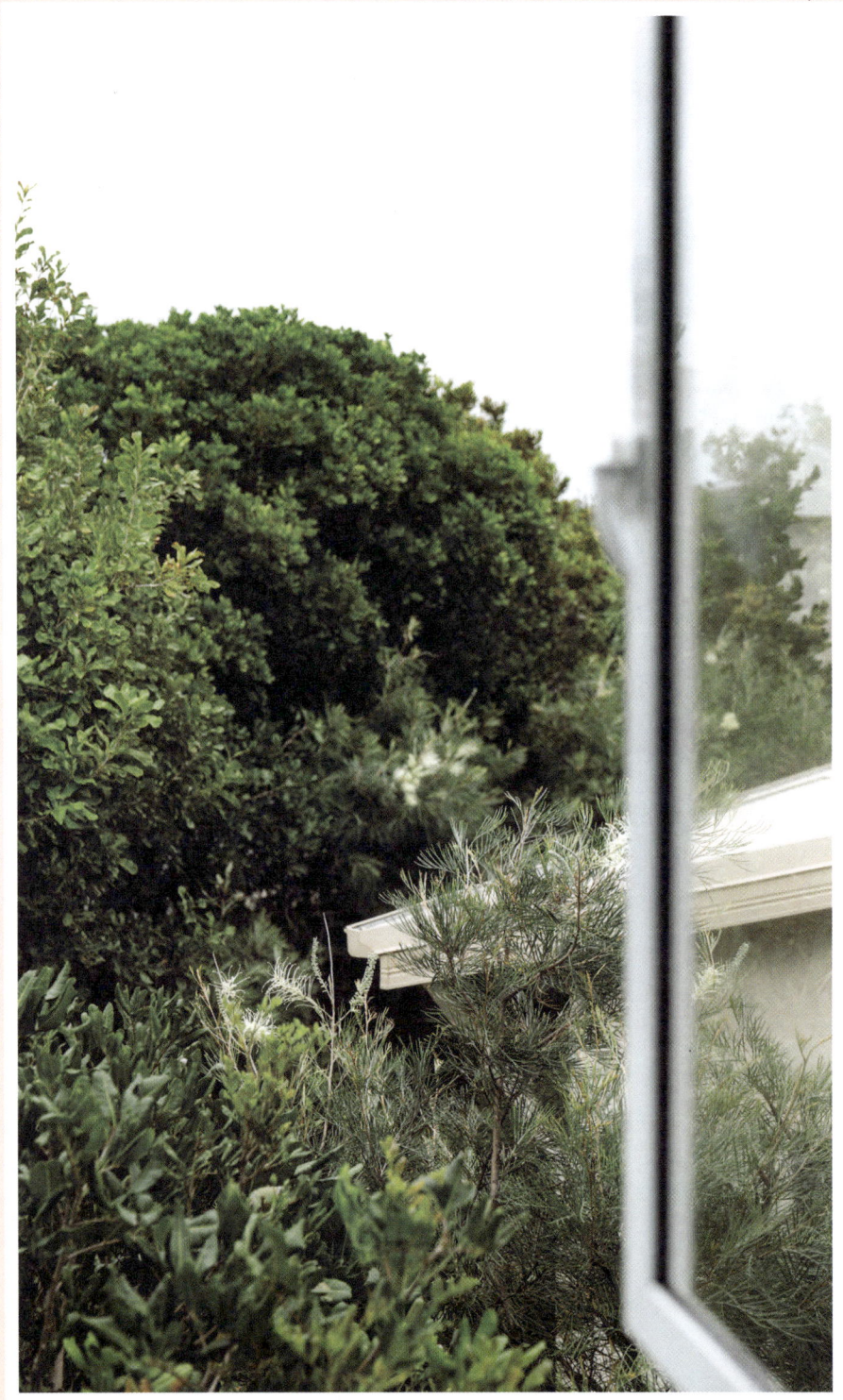

Supporting stomach acid production

So, if supporting your stomach acid production, and therefore your digestion, is going to help you decrease your invisible load, here are some ways to do this:

Chew.
Chew.
Chew.
Chew your food very well.

Eat slowly; chew everything in your mouth well and swallow it before the next mouthful goes in.

Drink water between meals, rather than with meals as water has a pH of 7 or greater and you don't want to risk diluting the stomach acid with its ideal pH of 1.9.

Apple cider vinegar or lemon juice in warm water 5 to 20 minutes prior to eating a meal can help to support stomach acid production.

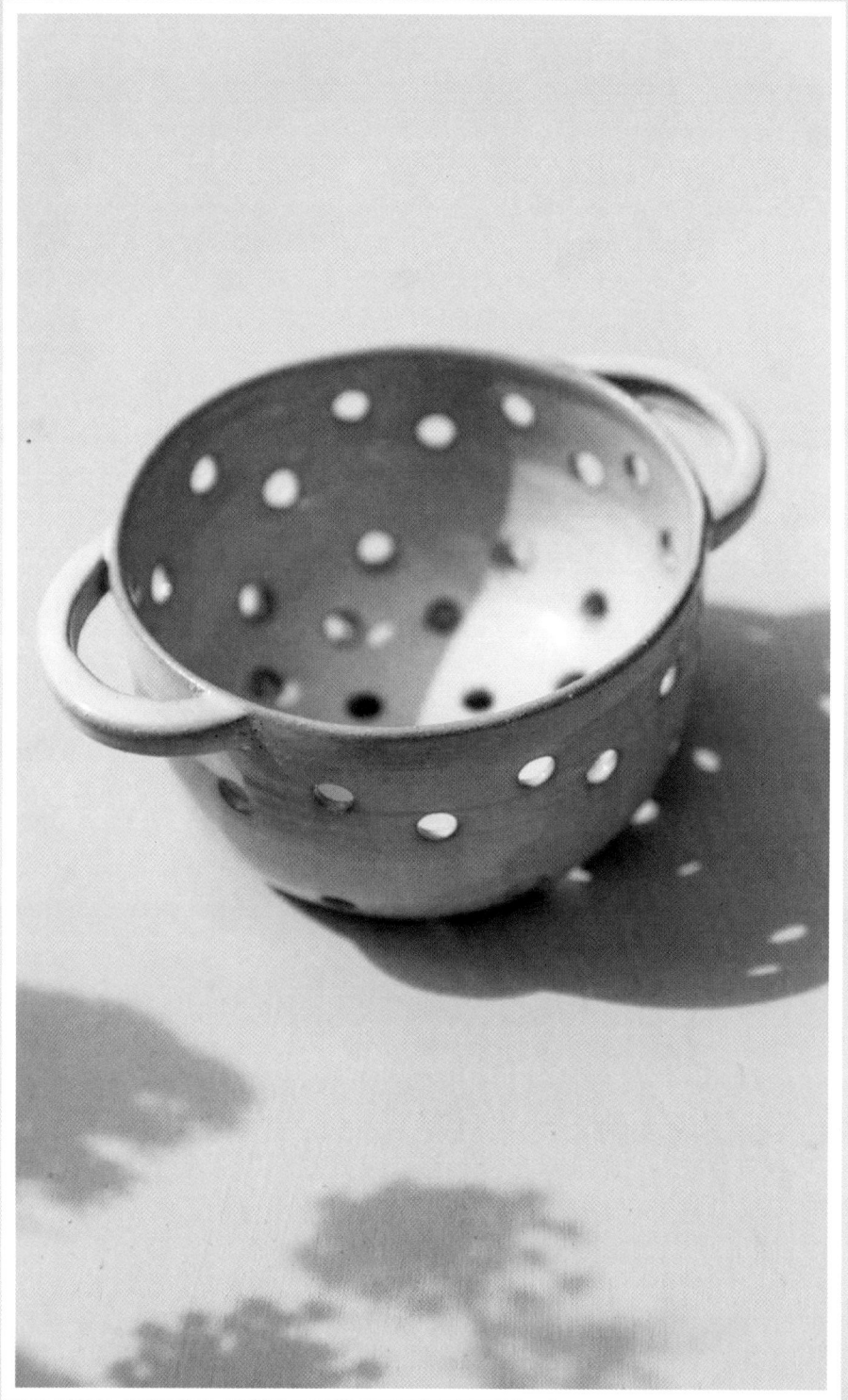

Leaks and gut bugs

Digestive overwhelm

One of the key consequences of digestive system overwhelm is leaky gut, or increased intestinal permeability as it is officially known. People might notice that when stress creeps into their lives and the load starts to build, their gut function changes. Symptoms such as bloating, excessive and/or offensive-smelling flatulence, diarrhoea, constipation or a feeling of incomplete evacuation begin to occur on a relatively regular basis. Irritable bowel syndrome (IBS) might also unfold, which is a topic all on its own in the next section.

How is it that leaky gut has become commonplace for too many people? To understand that, we first need to see how the lining of the gut appears and functions when it is working well. Small, finger-like projections called villi, upon which there are microvilli, extend from the lining of the small intestine.

They serve to increase the surface area of the small intestine so that nutrient absorption can be maximised, and they also serve as a location for some digestive enzymes.

Without the villi, food would zoom through here too rapidly and nutrient deficiencies result. In coeliac disease, before it is diagnosed and someone is still eating gluten, these villi are blunted and this is one of the reasons why some people's coeliac disease is found because of deficiencies in iron, zinc and/or vitamin B_{12}. Now that you know that, I need you to park that visualisation, as to keep this going makes it too complex to explain.

So, now imagine that what lines the tube that is the small intestine are neat rows of tightly packed bricks, top and bottom. The junctions between the bricks only allow nutrients to pass from the digestive system across into the blood. When the gut is leaky, the junctions have widened and larger substances can cross over into the blood. These larger substances might be fragments of food (microscopic but still too intact) and food is not supposed to be in your blood. Nutrients are. So, when a fragment of food ends up there, the immune system recognises it as something foreign, thinks it is a germ and mounts an immune response against it. This is one way adults can develop food sensitivities. This is not a true food allergy, but your body starts to react to foods you have eaten in the past without a problem.

The blood into which the food has crossed is the same blood that can flow to your brain. The blood–brain barrier is supposed to block the entrance of any problematic substances crossing over into the blood supply in the brain. But research has shown the fragments of food can end up binding to certain receptors in the brain. [1] Here's how.

In the brain we have what are called opioid receptors, which help to mediate whether we feel pleasure or pain. Opioid-based substances make us feel good and we can get attached or addicted to substances that give us a lift. Heroin and morphine, for example, are both opioids. The body produces its own feel-good substances, the best-known ones being endorphins. So when you get a lift in mood, whether it be from a Pilates session, watching the sunset or seeing your favourite bird, whatever spins your tyres drives your own production of endorphins. They bind to the opioid receptors in your brain and you get a lift in your mood.

A couple of foods can also do this, as their structures allow for them to become opioids if they are not digested properly. They are casein from dairy foods (known generally as beta-casomorphine) and gluten (known as gluteomorphin) from the gluten-containing grains. If these food fragments end up in the brain binding to opioid receptors, they don't elevate your mood in a way that makes you want to vibrantly celebrate, but they give you a feeling of needing them—so that if someone like me suggests you take a break from such foods, you might wish you'd never met me.

Please know, this binding in the brain doesn't occur for everyone. Two steps have to happen for this to occur. First, the protein fragment known as a peptide—in this case from casein and gluten—has to be not fully digested. Plus, the gut must have increased permeability. If only one of these factors has occurred, the food fragment cannot reach the brain.

If the peptide has been properly digested, it can no longer form an opioid-like structure. Or if the gut is not leaky, then even if the peptide forms, it cannot escape out of the gut and get into the blood, so therefore cannot reach the brain. This is just one tiny example of how much digestion matters.

HOW STRESS AFFECTS THE GUT

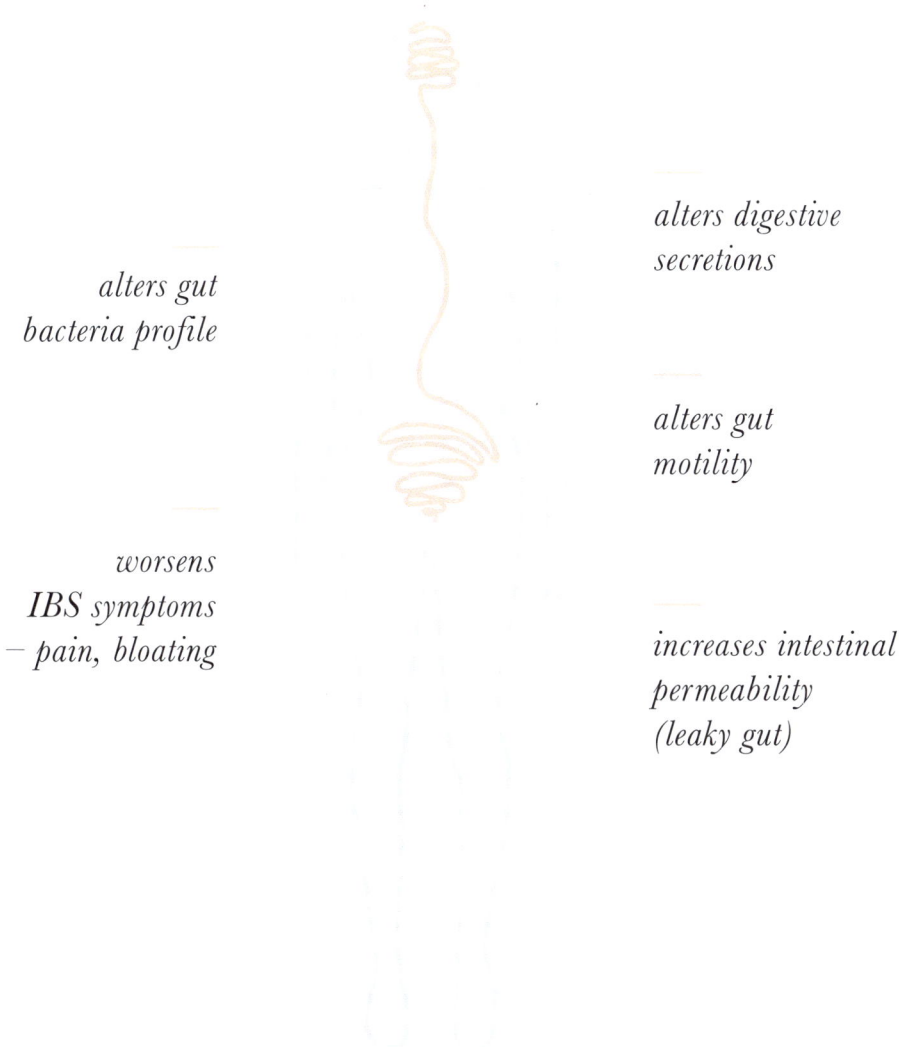

alters digestive secretions

alters gut bacteria profile

alters gut motility

worsens IBS symptoms – pain, bloating

increases intestinal permeability (leaky gut)

WHAT CAN LEAD TO A LEAKY GUT?

When we are born, our gut is leaky. It's just not referred to in this way as this is how it is supposed to be. By the time we are between two and five years of age, the junctions have become tighter and the lining of the gut looks like that of an adult. The age range when this occurs depends, in part, on what we go through with our health across those childhood years, and my opinion is that in some cases this can take longer to seal up and, in some children, fails to do so. But that is a conversation for another day.

A gastrointestinal infection at any age can lead to increased intestinal permeability. Take, for example, what is referred to generally as 'Bali belly'. You travel and pick up a parasite infection. You have diarrhoea for one or three weeks. That stops but your gut function is never the same again. The infection might initiate the leaky gut and then other factors can perpetuate it. Or for some a low-grade parasite infection—one that doesn't cause dramatic diarrhoea as occurred in the first instance—is what keeps the junctions too far apart. The food sensitivities follow soon after.

The third scenario that can lead to a leaky gut is constantly elevated stress hormones. In an attempt to help you save your life—remembering that this is what stress hormones think they've been made for—they try to increase the delivery of useful substances, such as nutrients, to the blood so you have a better chance of escaping or winning the fight. Many people today have relentlessly elevated stress hormone levels.

Yet another contributor to leaky gut are substances called lipopolysaccharides (LPS). These substances are found in the membrane of certain types of bacteria and some of them live in our gut. When there is too much LPS, intestinal permeability increases, [2] providing yet another example of how vital the gut bacteria profile—the microbiome—is to every inch of our health.

1 STRESS ITSELF

Not only can stress hormones increase gut permeability, but other aspects of the stress response can alter gut function. As mentioned on page 120, neurotransmitters like dopamine and serotonin, as well as noradrenaline and adrenaline, can act on gut motility and integrity. Think of athletes and how nerves before they race can send them off for an urgent trip to the loo with very loose stools— this is often the action of one or a multitude of these communication mediators at play. The same issues can occur in our day-to-day lives, with the SNS almost always being highly stimulated for too many people.

2 FOOD

There's no such thing as junk food. There is just junk and there is food. And up until the 'last paragraph' written in our 200-page book of human history, all we ate was food. And up until about 80 years ago, none of it was sprayed. We have all of the equipment inside ourselves to break down food. Substances like digestive enzymes act on what we swallow so we can extract nutrients and stay alive.

So, when we eat too much junk, we don't only miss out on the nutrients needed for life, but we also usually consume substances that are synthetic and that we have no ability to break down fully or substances that require detoxification before they can be eliminated, adding to digestive (and liver) overwhelm. Eat food, including plenty of plants. Not junk. And make water your main drink. These three things alone will go so very far towards decreasing the physical invisible load on your body, while also giving your mental health better opportunity to be well supported.

3 GUT FUNCTION, FOOD AND MENTAL HEALTH

Science is now starting to show what many have suspected to be true all along—that what we eat affects our mood. And that food impacts whether there are plenty of beneficial bacterial species, of diverse species, living in us as part of our microbiome, or not. A healthy gut microbiome has been linked to a greater ability to handle stress and a reduction in anxiety and a depressed mood.[*]

The brain-gut-microbiota axis (BGMA) is a communication system between your brain and your gut and the microbes within it, and the messages travel both ways. We still have much to learn about the precise mechanisms, and a question I'll keep an eye on having answered by new research over the coming years is whether the benefits come from the specific bacterial species themselves or substances they produce, perhaps vitamin-like substances or neurotransmitters, that help to regulate mood.

There may be other mechanisms at play, other than gut bacteria, through which nutritious food improves mood. Indeed, a 25 per cent increase in feelings of vitality and wellbeing was reported after only two weeks of improved dietary intake in a New Zealand study by young adults who increased their fruit and vegetable intake. [3] Two tiny weeks! This is significant in that it shows how rapidly our bodies respond when they receive what they need. Plus, when we feel more vital and alive the weight of our invisible load decreases and we tend to be better able to cope with what comes our way. That means it might take longer to feel overwhelmed or we can avoid going there at all.

Food, digestion, our microbiome and the BGMA are major players in our health. And the basis of what serves them well is incredibly simple. It's what we've always eaten—food, and in particular, plenty of plants. What, in the West, we now call whole real food. The rapid move away from what we, as a species, have always eaten has added a monumental rock to our packs and it's a rock you can, with focus and care, remove.

Dietary change is only one action among many steps people can take to improve mood and wellbeing. I am not suggesting it is a cure-all for major mental health diseases.

The irritated bowel

Linking stress and IBS

Irritable bowel syndrome (IBS) affects one in five Australians. It's twice as common in women as it is in men, often develops in the early twenties or even late teens these days and affects more women under 50 years of age than it does over this age. [1] The incidence is estimated to be even higher among New Zealanders. [2]

IBS can be the bane of someone's life. It can feel as though their gut will never function well again, that it will always give them grief. Common symptoms include bloating, cramps, pain, mucus in the stools, diarrhoea, constipation or intermittent bouts of both and excessive amounts of wind.

Years ago, as part of my clinical practice, I started asking an additional question when investigating someone's gut health and that was 'do you experience incomplete evacuation?' People with IBS would immediately know what I'm talking about when I would ask this and respond emphatically 'yes'. Those who don't have gut problems would have to pause to think about what I'd just asked. People with IBS often report a relief from bloating and pain after defecating and/or passing a lot of wind.

Over my years of clinical practice, I met countless women who suffered terribly with typical symptoms of IBS. After blood tests for coeliac disease, endoscopies and colonoscopies, they would be told that all results were negative, there was no sinister disease (relief) but that there was no explanation for their symptoms so it 'must just be in their head'. It is very disconcerting for a woman when she is led to feel that she doesn't know her body best—it breeds a destructive mistrust in herself and her relationship with her body that has long-lasting ramifications.

> IT IS VERY DISCONCERTING FOR A WOMAN WHEN SHE IS LED TO FEEL THAT SHE DOESN'T KNOW HER BODY BEST.

It is also upsetting when she feels there is no help at hand. Thankfully, recognition of the impact of IBS on quality of life and treatment protocols have vastly improved in recent years and there is light at the end of the tunnel for many. Don't stop until you get your answers. There is a reason behind everything you experience with your body, including IBS.

WHAT'S BEHIND IBS AND WHAT HELPS IT?

There is a chance that IBS, as we currently discuss it, is an umbrella term for numerous different mechanisms that have gone awry with the gut that we cannot yet distinguish. Or perhaps it is all just one condition—time and research will tell. A number of the neurotransmitters might be involved—serotonin and dopamine, for example—or much of it might be down to noradrenaline and adrenaline and their actions on the gut. It might be based on a mechanism or numerous mechanisms we are yet to fully understand involving the GBMA or the microbiome on its own, with some changes in these having already been noted in people with IBS. [3]

THE PRACTICALITIES

Here's what I've seen in clinical practice. My gut work taught me a catchphrase that I now use in every other aspect of my work: 'the road in is the road out'. In other words, whatever led to the problem has to be corrected for the person to experience a relief from or complete resolution of their symptoms. Here's what I witnessed make a difference for those with IBS, plus some extra things that I suspect are playing a role!

INFECTION

Often with a parasite if the gut symptoms started after a bout of food poisoning or travel diarrhoea, where you may have consumed water or food washed in water that you hadn't

had before, or undercooked meat, the first step to resolving the gut symptoms is to weed the gut of any nasties that may still be living in there. It may be a parasite, for example, and I have had many patients over the years test negative to parasites on a stool test but have symptoms completely resolve after treatment for parasites.

The herbs I would typically use include Chinese wormwood and black walnut for eight weeks. Often symptoms improve after about three weeks, but some parasites lay eggs so when they hatch the symptoms return if you've stopped treatment. That's why the eight weeks matters—to break their life cycle. Use of herbal medicine to treat the gut is best guided by an experienced practitioner.

OVERGROWTH OF STREPTOCOCCUS

There are bacterial species that use oxygen (aerobes) and those that don't (anaerobes). And of the bacteria in the large intestine, the majority of the aerobes are supposed to be *Escherichia coli* (*E. coli*). However, too many people these days have very little *E. coli* and an overgrowth of *Streptococcus*, or Strep as I refer to it. Some species of Strep do good things for us: some have been shown to produce a range of B vitamins, for example.

However, there are many challenges that arise when an overgrowth occurs, one of which is that Strep is a lactic acid-producing species. When there are too many of this species, and they produce too much acid, it changes the pH of the local environment which can make it inhospitable to other more beneficial bacteria.

THE FIRST STEP TO RESOLVING THE GUT SYMPTOMS IS TO WEED THE GUT OF ANY NASTIES THAT MAY STILL BE LIVING IN THERE.

Specific strains of Strep cause ear infections, tonsillitis and sinusitis, and they are often involved in pneumonia and bronchitis. Children particularly, but also adults, swallow the bugs when they are sick and stomach acid is supposed to sterilise what enters the stomach. However, as you learnt on page 121, for too many people, their stomach acid pH may still be acidic (pH less than 7) but not acidic enough to not only digest food well but for the critical sterilisation work to occur effectively. So, the Strep gets through and can take up residence in the large intestine and exert its disrupting effects. If this happens when we are very young, as it does for far too many children these days with recurrent ear infections, the immune system appears to develop a level of tolerance to Strep species, which can lead to lifelong immune and digestive-system challenges.

On top of that most people who have had chronic ear infections or tonsillitis growing up were given courses of antibiotics, further altering gut bacteria profiles. In my experience, this health picture does well on a strict dairy-free way of eating (it's not an allergy, but initially you need to eat like it is an allergy—super strict avoidance), supplemental vitamin C, zinc and stints of immune-supporting medicinal herbs such as echinacea.

FOOD REACTIONS

The words 'food allergy' and 'food intolerance' are used incorrectly everywhere these days. But rather than making this a discussion about such semantics, I'll stick to the topic of IBS and simply refer to an adverse response to the ingestion of a food as a 'food reaction' or 'food sensitivity'.

Food sensitivities/reactions that occur for someone diagnosed with IBS are not food allergies. For reasons that are not well understood, some people have a resolution of IBS symptoms when they omit certain foods. I have always encouraged this to be seen as a trial as it is likely that when the gut heals, they will tolerate these foods again, although not always.

IF THE BASIS OF THE IBS
SYMPTOMS IS EMOTIONAL,
RATHER THAN PHYSICAL,
THEN NOTHING RESOLVES
UNPREDICTABLE BLOATING
AND GUT SYMPTOMS LIKE
BEING WHO YOU ARE,
NOT FEARFUL OF WHAT
OTHERS THINK.

COMMON FOODS OR ASPECTS OF FOOD THAT PEOPLE WITH GUT PROBLEMS OFTEN DO WELL WITHOUT FOR A PERIOD OF TIME, OR LONG TERM, INCLUDE:

Dairy foods and, for some, this means all foods from the udder of any animal. For others, it is just cow's milk dairy. This may be due to poor casein digestion, lactose intolerance, the formation of casomorphines (see page 128), or mechanisms we don't yet understand. Clinically, though, many people's symptoms resolve with a dairy-free way of eating.

Gluten-containing grains which include wheat, rye, barley, oats and triticale. A test for coeliac disease is the only way we can currently assess whether someone digests gluten well or not. But there are likely numerous other mechanisms through which we might react to gluten. Or there may be other aspects to these food reactions that might be related to pesticide use or parts of the grains other than gluten, such as fructans.

Before I restrict any of the above, **artificial everything** has to go—sweeteners, flavours, colours, preservatives. Do you think preservatives are added to packaged foods to help you in any way? No, they are there to extend shelf life and they do that by inhibiting the growth of bacteria. And, as you know, your gut is teeming with bugs, most of them beneficial, or at least commensal, we hope!

It has always been common sense to my brain that something designed to prevent the growth of bacteria in food would impact our own innate populations and preliminary research is now suggesting that this is the case. [4] These preservatives—the sulphites—are commonly found in dips, dried fruit and wine and they destroy certain species of beneficial bacteria at concentrations considered safe for food. [4]

Based on the person's history, I would sometimes **trial a period without any fruit**. If complete resolution of symptoms occurred, I would then do trials to work out if it is all fruit or just some.

I would also trial the timing of fruit consumption. Some people feel better only eating fruit on an empty stomach first thing in the morning, whereas if they eat it for afternoon tea their symptoms will return. Others suffer with reactions to fruit any time they eat it.

When I started practising, the dietary approach that has become known as **FODMAPs** (explained below) had not been deciphered. I would simply play detective and observe patterns in my patients. Over time I came to find that many people with IBS needed to avoid only onion, garlic and apples (foods which are very high in certain FODMAPs) for management of their symptoms.

We now know that a modified FODMAPs way of eating has been shown to be very helpful for those with gut-based health challenges, particularly IBS. It doesn't cure IBS, but it can be highly beneficial for managing symptoms. FODMAPs is an acronym referring to substances in foods that can be poorly absorbed and then ferment and cause symptoms in some people. The letters stand for fermentable, oligosaccharides, disaccharides, monosaccharides and polyols. If the molecules are poorly absorbed in the small intestine, they continue their journey along the digestive tract, arriving at the large intestine, where they act as a food source for the bacteria living there. The bacteria then ferment the FODMAPs, causing the symptoms of IBS. This process also happens in people without IBS, although they don't have the increased gut sensitivity that IBS sufferers have. The fermentation action of gut bacteria on FODMAPs can also be one reason why some people feel better without fruit, or with only small amounts of specific fruits, when they have gut-based symptoms. Please note that this way of

eating is highly restrictive, particularly of fruits and vegetables, and must be guided by a qualified nutrition professional experienced in this area, as there are stages to the trial to determine what you can and can't tolerate. It is not wise to unnecessarily restrict fruits and vegies due to their immense health benefits (provided you digest them well). The low FODMAP phase itself is only designed to be followed for about two to six weeks, and it's essential that you're then guided through the next phase of reintroduction so that you're not unnecessarily restricting foods long term.

My preference is that one approach is trialled at a time. Otherwise, if you respond positively, you won't know what has done it. And all dietary trials are best done under the supervision and guidance of a qualified and experienced nutrition professional.

To have even the beginning of an understanding of how the gut works, a minimum of three years at university studying science truly is required. The gut is complex and our understanding of how it works is constantly changing as research teaches us more.

WHEN THE GUT DYSFUNCTION STEMS FROM STRESS

Gut function can become challenged when we live in a constant state of being overwhelmed, carrying an invisible load for too long. For many, it is one of the first places their state of SNS dominance shows up. And for too many, this is the work they resist. Or don't do. Or they put it off.

It's the hardest one to tackle, yet as with most things that are difficult, incredibly worthwhile. In other words, for some people, there is no amelioration of symptoms until they get to the heart of what is really behind their stress.

Stress might originate from trauma or huge amounts of change all at once, even more so if you don't see the changes coming. The body might start presenting gut-based symptoms after a relationship break-up, whether you instigated it or not. It might come from unrelenting worry about your finances and mortgage repayments, demands at work or the overwhelming concern about the health of someone you love.

Perhaps it all changed when someone or a pet passed away. Or it might be worry about school or university grades, troubles with friend groups, a debilitating body consciousness and/or a deep, deep fearfulness about what others think of you. Or a million other scenarios.

I have found that many people are prepared to do or even enjoy the dietary work and they will try every new dietary trend that pops up in an attempt to resolve the gut symptoms. And some days, or even weeks, this new approach might seem to work, but then out of seemingly nowhere, the symptoms are back, even though their food intake has not changed. This might be showing you a deeper emotional pattern or belief that you now have the opportunity to explore.

Sometimes closure from emotional pain simply requires time. And as more time passes from what happened, the symptoms will resolve. We sometimes think closure is all about words when, sometimes, time itself is a great healer.

And in the meantime, remain gentle and kind to yourself with how you eat, how you think and how you live. Of course, there are still steps you can take from a dietary perspective, as mentioned above. You don't just sit around suffering while you wait for time to pass!

For others, particularly those whose stress and gut symptoms stem from a damaging self-perception, rather than something happening, the deeper work usually heals so much more than just your gut. You find yourself almost being distilled back to who you really are, rather than who you think you need to be in order to be loved or gain approval.

If the basis of the IBS symptoms is emotional, rather than physical (related to microbiome changes, poor stomach acid production or food, for example—although of course it can be all three), then nothing resolves unpredictable bloating and gut symptoms like being who you are, not fearful of what others think.

Yoga has been shown to help IBS [5] and a study conducted comparing gut-directed hypnotherapy with dietary change and their impact on IBS found similar efficacy between the two interventions. [6] Both of these research pathways suggest stress plays a role in IBS, something I have witnessed first-hand as a practitioner.

ONE MORE THING

I cannot help but add this observation. IBS doesn't always stem from changes in gut integrity or the microbiome or a stressful event. For some girls, it starts when they move in with their boyfriend, something that is seemingly joyful for them. But when young women start cohabiting with someone they love, they usually stop passing wind. They hold it in in fear he will hear it or that it will have an odour.

And so the bloating starts. Then they start to stress that they are fat and then they start to eat less or in a finicky way trying to lose the weight they think they've gained. Then this ripples into more and potentially other anomalies in the state of the gut. But it started with not passing the gas that is naturally produced in the gut. On the surface, you have to deal with the practicality of passing wind. But behind the scenes, what's going on? She is terrified of not being loved and of being rejected, whether she is aware of this or not. In every ounce of work I've ever done, this ultimate fear is at the heart of just about everything. Probably everything, but I feel closed to learning if I don't stay open to other possibilities of what's behind … everything.

Remember you always have a choice. You have a choice to believe your stressful thoughts, or you have a choice to question them. If you'd prefer to live with more inner peace, I wholeheartedly encourage you to bring more curiosity to them.

DR LIBBY

Unpacking your body load

Calming techniques

Whether you enjoy or resent the heck out of the amped up, fast-paced version of life that has become the norm for many people in the Western world, your nervous system needs some time where there is less sympathetic activation and more parasympathetic activation. Your adrenal glands need some time where they are not on the receiving end of instructions that demand they produce stress hormones relentlessly. Not just for their own sake, but because of the flow-on effects you now understand stress hormones generate.

Ultimately, my desire for this book is to support you not just with practical strategies that lead to each body system and organ, like the digestive system, the adrenals, the pituitary and the ovaries, being less overwhelmed and carrying less of a load, but also to offer ideas about how to explore HOW you think. My goal with the latter is that you can spend less time with the stress tap having burst a water main and more time with the tap off or at least reduced to a minimal drip.

Yet, of course, there are times when the stress hormone tap will be turned on and we need strategies to lower stress hormones so that our health suffers less. Here are some ideas.

SLOW, DIAPHRAGMATIC BREATHING

Because we cannot consciously control the ANS, the only way we can have any influence over it is via how we breathe. When we breathe in a short, sharp, shallow way that only moves the upper part of our chest, adrenaline is in the driver's seat and this way of breathing continues to promote more stress hormone production. Historically we would only produce adrenaline, and subsequently breathe in this way, when our life was in danger and we have not yet evolved for this scenario to mean something other than that. Hurry up, evolution!

So, when we slowly and diaphragmatically breathe, we communicate to every cell in our body that we are safe, as we would never be able to breathe this way if our life truly was in danger.

Nothing that we currently know of lowers stress hormones faster than this style of breathing.

How do babies breathe? In and out through their nostrils and their little tummy goes up and down. Yet walk into a room full of adults and most of them will be displaying the upper chest breathing driven by stress hormone output, after years of conditioning this pattern. You keep yourself in SNS dominance, even though you are perfectly safe, when you breathe like this. So, the hypothalamus lets the pituitary know you're not safe and she sets the cascading stress response in motion. All from the way you breathe.

When you breathe diaphragmatically, when you inhale, your tummy (lower abdomen) pushes forward and when you exhale your tummy shrinks back towards your spine. You inhale slowly through your nostrils and don't hold your breath but just momentarily pause. Then slowly exhale through your nostrils. Ideally the exhalation is even slower than the inhalation.

Once you have mastered the connection of your breath with your lower abdomen, you can take it further and as the inhalation pushes the tummy forward, allow the breath to also move up into the ribcage and expand it out in all directions, especially sideways. The exhalation is the same—long and slow—and the air deflates out of the ribcage area first, and out of the tummy last of all.

This is the type of breathing, or a pattern similar to this, you'd be encouraged to do in a yoga or meditation class. So by all means embrace a regular breath-focused practice. You will receive other immense benefits from these practices as well. However, if they don't appeal, you don't have to actively participate in them to receive the benefits of diaphragmatic breathing. You can set yourself daily rituals where you do 20 long, slow breaths—when you are stopped at red traffic lights, every hour on the hour at your desk, first thing in the morning and last thing at night.

Be patient with yourself as it can take weeks before all of the parts of you respond to this new way of breathing. I've met countless women who cannot initially get their tummy to move with their breath as they've been sucking it in for most of their adult life! So it can take a while before everything feels connected again. Be patient with yourself. Embrace a daily breathing ritual. It can truly help you feel like your backpack weighs much less.

REDUCE CAFFEINE

Caffeine binds to receptors in the brain that then send a message to the adrenals to produce adrenaline. We cannot override this. This is the simple biochemistry of caffeine. And remember it is not just the adrenaline production that is the challenge here. It is the ripple effects that adrenaline drives where so many of people's health consequences originate. So whenever I see a study that shows the benefits of coffee—it can help with bile production for example—my fall-back position is that everyone is different. There are many men and women whose adrenaline levels are already through the roof and their chemistry simply cannot handle their adrenaline levels going any higher. We'll find other ways to stimulate their bile! A patient shared with me that her five-year-old can notice when she's had coffee as he links it to her impatience. After eight weeks off it to help with her menstrual cycle, she went back to one a day. His comment about how snappy she was now that she was drinking coffee again stopped her in her tracks. And yet some people don't get into a spin after one cup at all. It might take the second one or the fourth. I will never tell you in a blanket way how much is okay to have or whether you need to avoid it. It is highly individualised and it can change over time and with our life stages. It does drain minerals from you, and it does block the absorption of some nutrients so if you drink it, have it 30 minutes away from food and keep your consumption low enough so that it doesn't push you into a place where your anxious or flustered feelings hurt you.

My clinical experience shows me that a lot of women go through periods in their lives where they are better off without coffee. Then there are stages where they have less on their plate, more aspects of life feel predictable—the 14-year-old family member who shouted his way through his teens is now 17 and he's stopped shouting, for example. So many facets of life lead people to make adrenaline and when they become fewer, you usually handle coffee better.

Just have awareness—an honest awareness—about how it might be affecting you and then take steps to act on that if you know in your heart of hearts that you need to reduce it or have a period of time without it.

STILLNESS THROUGH MOVEMENT

Almost a decade ago, I was fortunate to have an experience of a practice that led to a deeper rest and level of calm than I had experienced through any other practice. It is called *Stillness Through Movement (STM)* and it was created by Tracy Whitton. Part of the practice involves lying in yoga poses supported by bolsters and weighted down with blankets. Your body has nothing to do except its essential processes (breathing, heart pumping blood, for example). This combination of support and weight, plus the breath focus of this practice, activates the PNS and dampens down the SNS more effectively than anything else I've experienced. The pituitary gland must finally do a deep breath herself during this practice because finally she is not having to put out the fires created by the SNS. The website for this truly restorative practice is: www.stmt.com.au.

MEDITATION

Meditation means different things to people. For some it is a breath-focused, restorative practice while for others it is a spiritual practice. For many, it is both. Its health benefits are now widely recognised and it genuinely helps to simplify your life. Ram Dass expressed it beautifully when he said: 'As you enter quieter spaces you will see how clinging to desires has made your life complicated. Your clinging drags you from desire to desire, whim to whim, creating more and more complex entanglements. Meditation helps you cut through this clinging.' Meditation can help to encourage you to simplify your life and see into what feels impenetrable to change, opening up possibilities that you couldn't otherwise glimpse.

WHOLE, REAL FOOD

Nothing in this world can replace a real-food way of eating. No amount of exercise can ever counteract the effects of a lousy diet. Besides the stress response itself, you learnt earlier about the impacts of oxidative stress, a damaging and ultimately debilitating process that occurs when you consume too few antioxidants, found predominantly in coloured plant foods. Please eat plenty of vegetables.

Remember that there is no such thing as junk food. There is just junk and there is food. And your Earth Suit had only ever eaten food, up until the very, very, very, very … recent past, when the junk infiltrated the food supply. As Michael Pollan so succinctly said: eat food, not too much and mostly plants.

Minerals are needed to allow muscles to literally be able to relax—specifically magnesium and calcium. Green leafy vegetables, nuts and seeds are our major sources of dietary magnesium, while calcium is widely spread throughout many whole, real foods, including sesame seeds, tahini, almonds, figs, green leafy vegetables, salmon with edible bones and sardines.

Do what you can to make as much of your food organic. Again, up until the 1940s that's all there was. We don't fully know how we might be affected by the long-term consumption of a mixture of pesticides, but what is occurring with low sperm counts is a potentially concerning sign. Before the 40s food was organic. So it would have been more accurate to continue to refer to what is now labelled as 'organic food' as 'food' and the conventional produce of today as 'sprayed food'. Choose organic wherever you can. Do what feels comfortable—and then see if you can stretch a little.

NATURE

Being among trees and mountains hearing nothing but birdsong, or at the beach, or witnessing the wide open plains stretching out in front of you with the biggest sky you've ever seen, nourishes us in indescribable ways. Not only do we likely breathe more slowly in these environments, but when all you are focused on is the way the bird you are watching is playing on the breeze, there is often a joy to be felt and stresses are laid to rest, even if only momentarily. There's a

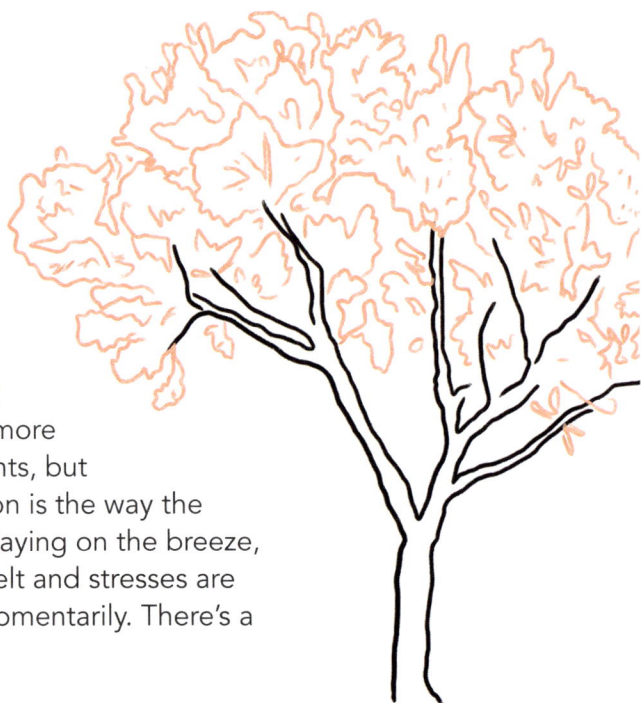

calm that can wash over you more easily beholding such vistas and a reminder of what's important to you; what you really care about tends to bubble more easily to the surface.

If you live in a city, perhaps find a green pocket to immerse yourself in each lunchtime or take regular trips out of the city on the weekend. Less noise, less being asked of you, plenty of oxygen, movement of your body and observation of natural processes can help to reconnect you to healthy patterns and perceptions. Up until the very recent past we lived as part of nature and our nervous system is calmed by familiar surroundings and her simplicity and beauty. The rhythms of nature offer calmness, clarity and remind you to trust yourself.

ORDER

Having structure and order in our spaces can also support calm. Yet sometimes the thought of tackling the overhaul of a cupboard or drawer or whole room can add to the overwhelm. Less clutter, less stuff and more open space can assist our brains (and the Earth) to not be funnelled into a spiral of chaos so often. Or perhaps you like lots of knick-knacks around you to prompt happy memories so it's the bathroom cabinet or the cutlery drawer in the kitchen where you'd prefer your order.

Or maybe your focus becomes your work space at home and/or the office. An orderly desk that you appreciate the appearance of, tidy drawers, or perhaps its old emails filed into folders at the end of each week. Sometimes our brain can think more clearly when there is a degree of order in our surroundings. You can't always overhaul everything at once so contemplate what you could work towards bringing more order to.

In saying all of that, there are stages in our lives where mess is unavoidable unless you want to spend every waking hour cleaning up—umm, no thanks.

So applying the Serenity Prayer (refer to page 243) to a busy home where young children live (for example) can sometimes be the best road to calm! Or just embrace the mess, if that nourishes your soul, with an awareness that you are doing this, so you don't pass silent judgement on yourself when you observe the mess. It can be a great feeling when what might be chaos at home brings a grin to your face.

HERBS

Medicinal herbs can also assist the stress response. They work in a variety of ways; however, the use of herbs is best guided by a qualified medical herbalist (you can read about the Dr Libby clinic at www.drlibby.com). There are adaptogenic herbs that help to modulate the stress response and support adrenal gland function, while others have a calming action. Herbs to consider to assist with calm as well as the stress response include skullcap, lemon balm, chamomile, zizyphus, withania (ashwagandha), Siberian ginseng, liquorice, paeonia, rehmannia, rhodiola and tulsi (Holy basil).

PERCEPTIONS

Without opening this can of worms completely, consider your perception of how you expect life to be. Many people I've spoken to, for example, expect to have no problems. So, when they do experience them, even the smallest thing overwhelms them. Or perhaps you expect your business to run smoothly yet a huge part of most businesses involves solving problems. The problem is in the perception or the belief that you aren't supposed to have any.

How do you perceive your emails? The bane of your life, you feel like you constantly let people down as you can't reply to them promptly enough, and you just can't keep up? Or do you see an opportunity in every email? The first scenario you can see will generate a stress response, while the second one won't. Do you expect to have an up-to-date inbox, even though you've had only two occasions in the past five years when this has occurred? I am no email inbox chaos

resolver (other than knowing folders help my brain) but rather want to prompt you to consider how you perceive them and how your inbox is supposed to look. Empty is not possible for most of us, which is only a problem if you think it needs to be another way. Many jobs require us to be efficient certainly, but this won't always mean empty.

How do you perceive control? Do you believe you are in charge of your life, that you have any control, or do you spend your day desperately wishing for more control over things? Some of our stress gets set up by our relationship with and how we perceive control. More on this on page 267.

HOW DO YOU PERCEIVE CONTROL? DO YOU BELIEVE YOU ARE IN CHARGE OF YOUR LIFE, THAT YOU HAVE ANY CONTROL, OR DO YOU SPEND YOUR DAY DESPERATELY WISHING FOR MORE CONTROL OVER THINGS?

Our perception of freedom is another area which, if not examined wisely, can lead to an ongoing stress response. Freedom means so many different things to people. For some it is connected to where they live—a free country, or not. While for others freedom might be highly linked to choice. More choices equals more freedom in their belief system. And all myriad scenarios in between. An exercise I used to do with clients to help them examine why they drank alcohol every night was to ask them to finish the sentence 'wine is…' (or replace 'wine' with whatever their drink was). And after a while you get to the bottom of what it is and for some it is freedom. It represents their freedom. Yet in some of these situations the person had lost their freedom with alcohol. It now owned her. In this instance, she needs to connect things other than alcohol to her freedom so she can still feel free, but not hurt herself (and potentially others) in the process. How do you perceive freedom?

I encourage you to ask yourself what calms you and perhaps explore why. Note them down and then work out how you can incorporate more that fosters calm for you. Or it might be that what you do doesn't need to change for you to have more calm. It's HOW you do it that will change the game.

Soul food

SUNSETS

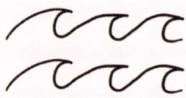

SWIMMING
IN THE SEA

YOGA

LISTENING TO
YOUR FAVOURITE
SONG ON REPEAT

EMBRACING
YOUR INNER
ARTIST

LAUGH AT
BAD JOKES

MAKE A
PICNIC

HAVE A
BUBBLE BATH

READ A BOOK

Simple ways to release the stress and welcome the calm.

GO FOR
AN ADVENTURE

SPEND TIME
BY YOURSELF

CUDDLING UP
TO YOUR PET

GARDENING

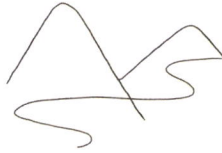

WALK IN
NATURE

WATCH YOUR
KIDS PLAY

CRAFTERNOON

HUGGING
A TREE

VOLUNTEER
FOR A CHARITY

Four simple destress hacks

For when you're on the stress express

CHECK YOUR LANGUAGE

The language we use really matters. The words you choose to convey what you think and feel don't just impact those who hear what you are saying. Your own body has a response to the language you choose. Think of the word 'flow'. What arises? There's often a relaxation response, an 'ah' sound as your breathing naturally slows or deepens. The words 'stress' and 'anxiety' often do the opposite. You might like to even notice what's there for you when you read a word, let alone say it out loud. The word 'overwhelm' can foster a similar response. Yet if you examine what these words actually are, they are a host of biochemical responses that drive a change in your physiology and your psychology. So, when it comes to your language choices, you might like to replace the words you notice evoke a heightened response in you—such as stress perhaps—with the word 'energy' and observe how this leads you to feel. If 'energy' doesn't fit with how you feel, try 'busy' and see if this down-regulates the stress response somewhat. Play with the words you use, as they can add to an already amped-up state or they can contribute to calming you down.

GET MOVING

As you've already learnt, adrenaline, cortisol and the amount of glucose in your blood all escalate when the SNS is stimulated. All of it is to help you escape from the danger that your body perceives you are in. We've talked about how the stress hormones drive changes in your heart rate and even blood flow to give you more chance of survival and the glucose increases to give you a much-needed fast-burning fuel to get out of there. Yet what happens when there's nothing to actually run from? What is on offer to you when you are in this heightened state? While, for some, their fatigue from the ongoing stress response is endless, others are filled with energy, and if there's energy, there's usually plenty of it, because you need to fight or to flee.

Although this book is about understanding stress, your invisible load, and ways to get to the heart of what is really driving your stress responses, this can take time to unravel. Plus, there are sometimes occasions when we simply need to either utilise or quell what's on offer. To do the latter, you've come to learn about how powerful long, slow exhalations are in reducing the sympathetic activation that has occurred to get us into this state in the first place, and at stimulating the PNS. But another option is to utilise the energy on offer to you as this too can mop up the effects of the stress hormones. Exercise, movement of any kind, outdoors or even housework—vacuuming never felt so good!—can all help to return your body to homeostasis. I'll add a caveat here. For those who are in stage 3 stress (discussed on page 67), breath-focused restoration is a much more supportive choice than vigorous activity. For those in stage 1 or 2 of the stress response, feel free to go for it and use that energy.

LEGS UP THE WALL

A yoga pose, technically known as Viparita Karani, also referred to as 'legs up the wall', is highly calming and restorative. You can do it on the floor with your legs up the wall, or on your bed with your legs up the bed head.

A simple way to get into the position is to sit with one of your hips against the wall (so you are side on to the wall), and then as you twist to lie back onto your back, you swing your legs up the wall. Your bottom is positioned close in to the wall and your legs are straight, but comfortable up the wall. Your heels rest on the wall. You can put a folded blanket under your bottom or lower back if that feels more supportive and comfortable.

It also feels relaxing to open your arms out wide so they radiate out from your heart. You will usually effortlessly drop into diaphragmatic breathing when you get into this position. If not, bring your focus to your breath and breathe in through your nostrils, expanding your lower abdomen as you do. Gently pause after the inhalation and then slowly exhale through your nostrils as your tummy lowers back down towards your spine. This can be a particularly calming ritual to do for five to ten minutes before you go to sleep.

KITCHEN GROOVES

Energy begets more energy so another option when you are full of stress hormones is to turn up your favourite tracks and bust out some dance moves. Not only do you utilise the cascade of biochemical changes that adrenaline has driven, including the glucose it mobilises into your blood, but you get the physical and mental benefits of moving in this way. Plus, you tend to be left with an uplifted mood after a good dance around the kitchen that can persist into the coming hours!

Next time you find yourself having climbed aboard the stress express and are somewhat amped up for reasons you can or can't explain, employ one of these four additional (to diaphragmatic breathing and meditation mentioned on pages 147 and 150), stress-quelling options. Start to notice what makes a difference for you. And remember, it's often a series of small steps that will work together to reduce your invisible load.

Rings and pings

Turning down the volume on your overwhelm

With one of the themes of this book being about changing the things that we can and accepting what we can't change for now—and, yep, having some wisdom to decipher between the two—something to check in with yourself about is sound. Some sounds in our environment we can't change (hello traffic), while there are many that we can.

Do you thrive in situations where it is loud? Where there are competing sounds like multiple people talking and music playing and the television on and cutlery clanging? Or is that close to your worst nightmare? If so, then I encourage you to consider the impact everyday sounds (that you may have become accustomed to) have on you, particularly on your nervous system.

Do you have every notification activated on your phone so that it pings and dings and frog croaks and duck quacks to let you know when you have a new message in any of maybe six different vehicles of communication? What about when you are mentioned on a social media platform? Is there a sound every time you receive an email? If so, that can all add up to a barrage of sounds across the day.

If you thrive on noise or it doesn't bother you, of course set yourself up to receive every ping possible. But if you feel a little (or majorly) jolted every time your phone makes a sound, turn off the push notifications so that you only see them when you actively go into that app. Turn off the sounds, keep your phone on silent, disconnect emails and use your phone as a phone for calls and text messages, if that appeals, or any combo of these. Choose when you check Instagram rather than allowing a notification to prompt you. You may at first feel like you'll be less efficient. But all it means is that you deal with emails and direct messages when you choose to go there. Start to notice if you really do have to deal with things immediately and urgently or if you just make yourself feel like that. Some jobs certainly require things be attended to with haste, but not many. We've just made it normal to check emails and respond to notifications at all times of the day and night.

I encourage you to consciously establish HOW you use your phone and other devices in a way that, rather than add to your overwhelm, supports you and HOW you want to live. Experiencing fewer sounds might sound (pardon the pun) too simple to make a difference, but every little ounce of SNS stimulation can add up across our day. Look for these and other types of small ways that can help to take the edge off your overwhelm.

WAYS TO CUT DOWN YOUR RINGS AND PINGS

1. Ask yourself if you really need to take your phone with you wherever you go. For example, do you always need it with you on a walk, out for dinner or when you go to get groceries?

2. Manage all notification alerts in your settings. Better yet, remove the apps entirely and try to use your phone only for calls or texts. You can always log in to your emails or social accounts via the browser on your phone should you need to.

3. Put your phone on flight mode from 6 p.m. until 6 a.m. (or a period of time that works for you). This can help you to stop checking emails when you don't need to, which can be tempting even when you've muted notifications!

4. Set time limits on your apps. This can be monitored in your settings in 'Screen Time' (if you have an iPhone) or by using a phone usage app.

5. Avoid the temptation of putting the phone on the table beside you when you're eating a meal or in a meeting and leave it in your bag instead.

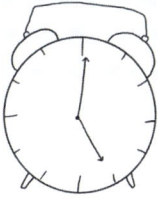

6. Get an alarm clock and move your phone out of your bedroom through the night. This can help to stop any unnecessary late night or early morning scrolling while also ensuring you aren't disrupted by any alerts through the night.

7. Tell your friends, family and work colleagues that you are not available after office hours (or whatever timeframe feels right for you) and won't be answering texts, calls or emails during those hours.

Some of these suggestions might not be practical for your needs. They are simply designed to act as a prompt to get you to consider where you can create some space for yourself from sounds and feeling as though you have to act with urgency. This can go a long way to reducing your invisible load.

MIND LOAD

My hope for this section of the book is that it offers you empathy and deep compassion. That it cultivates an immense kindness and patience in you for yourself, and others—for the stress in your life that is unwavering, invisible, unavoidable and real. I also hope it helps you to foster a new perspective for all the stress that your current thought patterns and beliefs create for you, which is in your power to change. After all, we are not our thoughts or our behaviours, although growing up people often merge the two and refer to who we are based on how we behave. Know that you are responsible for your behaviour but it doesn't define you, that your beliefs shape your world but they aren't the way things are and that all of us are the sum of our pains and joys in life up until now, so be gentle with yourself and everyone you meet.

The thread that unravels your stress

Changing what overwhelms you

For too long people have felt powerless to change the daily stress they experience. We have recited 'I'm so stressed' like a broken record inwardly or outwardly for a decade or far longer—feeling like there is nothing we can do to change it to give ourselves any relief. Or perhaps you don't identify with the word 'stressed' and instead your mantra is 'I'm worried' or 'I'm just overwhelmed with everything I have to do'. To the body, it's all the same.

We think we are stressed because of circumstances—all of that out there. The mortgage, the job, the work hours, the challenging colleague, the juggling act of full-time work, raising children, running a household and all the details these entail, being there for our partner, friends, family, the emails, the phone calls, the messages, the reports to be written … and the list of tasks and responsibilities large and small goes on and on and on.

There is no question that some of the things we refer to as stressful truly are. Yet, many more are the result of our perceptions—our view of our world and the view we have of ourselves. We just can't always see that when we are stuck in the middle of it all.

WHAT IS STRESS, REALLY?

I've come to see stress as essentially fear. It is a response to what happens when there is a lack of safety, or a perception that safety might be lost. Put another way, you knowingly or unknowingly perceive the existence of risk of a lack of safety.

Now, safety for humans is both physical and emotional. The physical risks are obvious. Some examples might be you are walking home late one night by yourself and someone starts following you, or a car drives out in front of you and you need to slam on your brakes. To explore what emotional safety is to us as adults, it might first be wise to explore what it is to a child.

To a child, safety is attention and having their needs responded to. In time, a growing human starts to call this love. The reason the need for love is hard-wired into us (into the ANS, explored on page 58) as human babies is because when we are born, we can't survive on our own the way other animals can. We need someone to care enough about us to provide food, clothing, shelter, warmth, and time in their arms to bring that sense of safety to our developing nervous system.

So, from an emotional perspective, safety becomes love to us, and we tend to want to please whoever we needed that from as children (whether they gave that to us or not). We do this because on some level as adults, we are still trying to secure and ensure our safety. In other words, for many people, emotional stress is what happens when we perceive there is a loss of love or we perceive that we risk losing love. Think about what happens inside your head or to your body when someone yells at you. Maybe you get defensive or maybe you just shrink. Maybe you feel physically ill or well up with tears. Whatever your reaction might be, consider why you react that way. Is it because you're frightened that it means they think less of you? Do you get defensive because you can't stand the thought that this person might be seeing you in an unfavourable light? It might take some reflection to get to the heart of your 'why', but if there is any reaction in you, there will be some kind of perceived risk to your safety. Because someone else's anger is just their anger—until we perceive that their anger means something about us.

As adults, we may (or may not) still want to make the adult/s who raised us happy by how we live our lives now or how our character traits appear to them. Quite often, the traits that we perceived pleased our caregivers in the past, or the behaviours that got us what we wanted, become part of who we perceive we need to be or how we act. This becomes the way we feel we need to appear to others in the outside world.

We all create our own identities as we are growing up in response to our environments. For example, maybe we get rewarded for good behaviour or are severely punished when we overstep a caregiver's house rules. Essentially, the gist is that we construct our identities in a way that we perceive gets us the most love or attention or helps us to avoid rejection from the adults in our lives. Behaviours that aren't necessarily so constructive can also be established during this time and from those behaviours we unconsciously make decisions about who we are. Our invisible loads get heavier as we strive to uphold the identities we create for ourselves, no matter the cost. For example, we might unknowingly 'learn' that we gain more attention if we misbehave. Or the adults in our lives might give in to what we want if we hassle them long enough. Or we might create drama out of not much at all in an attempt to gain attention. If these behaviours get set up when we are young, we might carry them into future relationships with partners or friends, if we don't do the inner work of understanding our choices and behaviours. Lousy behaviour can bring much stress to you and sometimes to those around you. It might be that we learned through observation while we were growing up that people get their way after a period of giving someone else the silent treatment. So now, as an adult, you might do the same, but given that it upsets those you love or causes conflict, you wish you wouldn't. We tend to construct our identities in response to what gained us the most 'safety' (love/attention) growing up. And if this behaviour is somewhat dysfunctional once we are an adult and we suffer as a result (it might lead to us not being able to maintain long-term relationships, for example), rather than suffer and complain (inside our heads or to others) we get the opportunity to dismantle it, bring immense compassion to ourselves for doing the best we could growing up the way we did, and live in a different way. It's not easy, but the rewards for you and for humanity are worth it.

RISKS OF A LOSS OF LOVE, SAFETY AND BEING VIEWED INCONSISTENTLY WITH OUR IDENTITY

Another area where stress can rear its head is when we experience a risk that there might be a potential loss of our emotional safety. It's the safety of being loved/liked/appreciated/admired/accepted when there is the chance we might come across as bearing a character trait that a parent/carer would not have approved of. In other words, when we run the risk of being perceived by another as something that it is so important for us NOT to be seen as. When something threatens our identity in this way, by golly does it stress us out. By lifting the veil on your invisible load and the stress you carry, you start to see that at their very roots, the things that stress us often stem from worrying about what other people think of you.

Let's get specific so you can start to see the truth for you in some of these stress responses, so you can begin to unravel them. Please know that when I talk about stress, I'm not referring to trauma, but rather what people share with me are their everyday stresses. These might typically include their to-do list, their email inbox, letting others down, ensuring loved ones feel valued, or running late.

WORRYING ABOUT INSTAGRAM?

As I mentioned earlier, when I asked women in their twenties what stresses them out, the two most common answers I received were their Instagram profile and posts, and their body. When I shared this at an event I spoke at, the audience, who were predominantly aged 40 and above, made audible noise that sounded to me like they were passing judgement on what stressed the younger generation out. So, I called them on it in a playful way and suggested that it is all the same. Isn't it possible that a 22-year-old worrying about her last couple of posts has a similar emotional landscape to a 45-year-old worrying about her overflowing email inbox and the meeting she is running late for? Both are potentially worried about being perceived as a failure, or not being accepted or liked, or thought of in a way that is incongruent with how they want to be seen—or some variation of this. It's just the many ways the patterns I'm describing play out and at different life stages: worrying about how others see us. If you weren't worried about how others see you, you wouldn't stress about these things—they'd just be part of your life.

FEAR

Stress can be a word people in the Western world use unknowingly as a cover for fear. It would sound quite odd to tell people that you are scared of your to-do list, although you may have joked about this at times. Let's unpack this a little further. Think about the last time you felt really worked up on the inside. You may not have shown it outwardly to anyone, but you were stressed—or worried or feeling pressured. Let's say it was because you were running late for a meeting. If this scenario caused you to feel some variation of stress, pause to consider what it might really have been about. Consider it this way: 'if stress is actually showing me something that I'm frightened of, what might that be?' What you'll see when you pull the curtains back on what stresses you out—in this case 'running late'—

is that most people are scared of what other people think of them when they act or behave in ways that might suggest to others that they're not reliable, dependable, trustworthy, honest, considerate, respectful—traits they can't bear to have associated with them.

If it is your email inbox that stresses you out, pause to consider why this might be, as emails don't overwhelm everyone. I used to ask my patients to tell me about their inbox during a consultation so I could gain some insight into their stress levels and their origins. Some people would just shrug their shoulders and comment that they were just emails. Others said they saw an opportunity in each email, while for others they'd share their despair at never being able to keep up. When the response was the latter, I'd ask more questions as there was clearly a stress response. If you feel like your emails are contributing to your invisible load and that you can't keep up, you might be worried what people will think if you don't reply to them promptly—that you are inefficient, disrespectful or don't care—which will be the opposite of the truth and the opposite to how you want to be seen. Otherwise you wouldn't stress about your emails. They'd still need attending to, but they'd just be what they are—your emails.

Or perhaps you bend over backwards to be there for and do as much as you can for others. You cannot say no, no matter how drowning in tasks and responsibilities you already are. So when every bone in your body is screaming at you to decline doing yet another thing and you find yourself saying that you'll help and regretting it afterwards, pause to consider how you fear being seen by the person who would be on the end of your no. It's likely you don't want to 'let them down' as this leads you to feel guilty, an emotion that is too familiar yet also uncomfortable for you and you probably can't bear to be seen as selfish or thoughtless. Yet, in your heart of hearts, do you believe the person who would be on the receiving end of your no would actually think this of you? If you were to let them know that you'd love to help but that you are swamped, do you honestly think

'IF STRESS IS ACTUALLY SHOWING ME SOMETHING THAT I'M FRIGHTENED OF, WHAT MIGHT THAT BE?'

they'd judge you? The opposite, more likely. They are more likely to show their care and concern for you and if they don't, it's unlikely they are a true friend anyway. People who help when they can, yet have no problem saying no when they need to, have flexibility rather than rigidity in how they can be seen by others. They might have a preference in how they are seen, but their self-worth is not tied to this.

Once you see the stress for what it really is, you can decide if you stay in that worked-up state or not, as now you can see the truth: you aren't stressed, you are concerned about what someone (or a group of people) thinks or might think of you. With this insight, you can pause and rationalise what's really bothering you about this scenario instead of futilely working yourself up into a state about something that is potentially not even in your control.

What are you worried that they'll think of you? How are you concerned that they will perceive you? It can be a very insightful process to start to name the traits in a journal you might like to keep as you explore what your stresses really are.

STAYING TRUE TO OUR CONSTRUCTED IDENTITY

Each individual has constructed an identity. And we will do anything to stay true to that identity. For wired into us is the fear that if we aren't seen how we 'need' to be seen, we risk losing love or respect, or any other word in the same genre as these. Perhaps liked or appreciated.

Here's how I see it. You have a word written across your forehead and it is so important to you that people view you in this way. You will do anything to remain congruent with that word, including sacrificing your own health (a concept I discussed in *Rushing Woman's Syndrome*). So, when you run late and that stresses you out (remember it doesn't stress everyone out), what character traits are you worried will be applied to you? And are they the opposite to how you want to be seen? Maybe you believe they'll see you as unreliable or flaky, for example. When you are exhausted and have run out of words at the end of your week, but said you'd go to a dinner with six others and every bone in your body is screaming 'Noooooooooo!', do you stress yourself out trying to decide whether to go or not? If you weren't concerned about what they thought of you, you'd just decide, rather than stress about it.

When you get yourself into this pickle, how are you worried they will see you? As selfish? Unreliable? Lacking in integrity? Most women will do almost anything to avoid risking being seen as 'selfish'. It goes against the very essence of how most of us were raised (being unselfish fosters caring and a sense of community). Yet, you can argue that you aren't acting in a selfish way to want a night to yourself after a busy week. In fact, you can argue the opposite—that you are being thoughtful not dragging your weary self to the dinner, risking being an energy vampire to the rest of the group. You can see it as the night in of self-care that you've needed all week and that it is selfish to deprive yourself of what you, your body and mind need.

No matter how you slice it, you won't put your much-needed downtime ahead of joining your friends if you don't have absolute certainty that they see you in a favourable light. If you don't know in your heart that they, or at least your favourite in the group, truly realises you are a wonderful person, a good human, you'll most likely go. If you don't know this, and you stay at home, you likely won't have any peace during your night in. Your thoughts will rattle around procuring all the guilt in the world, piling it up on top of yourself, leading you to feel like you've let them down and you are selfish after all. Your friends, by the way, if they are truly your friends, will not think this of you. The judgement you pass on yourself is far harsher than anything they will ever say or think.

Until you do the inner work, of unravelling what your stress really is for you, this is how it shows up and how it sits in the backpack of your invisible load. It's a cliché I know, but here it is anyway: it's not always easy to do this inner work, but it is beyond worth it to truly understand and appreciate yourself and who you really are. And you are magnificent, don't you worry.

FOREHEAD WORDS

What is drawn across your forehead? What traits are important to you and how do you prefer to be seen? Name them. On page 180 are some common examples that people have shared with me over the years…

You might like to take this a step further. When did this trait (or these traits) in you first begin? Do you recall? Remember, it usually develops in response to trying to please a parent or caregiver.

What arises when you ponder these concepts? You might start to see how parts of your personality have been constructed in response to the fear that you are not enough, not acceptable, not worthy (of being loved) unless you behave in a certain way. Many people mould themselves into who they feel they need to be to ensure they obtain

Playful • Sunshine • Peaceful • Wise • Respectful • Helpful

Kind • Thoughtful • Selfless • Perfect • Considerate • Lovely

Honest • Strong • Independent • Reliable • Efficient

Dependable • Supportive • Creative

love rather than just being who they are. So they develop masks that they wear. And they feel like they need to keep them plastered in place so that all people, particularly those whose opinions matter to them (whether they understand why they seem to care about what others think of them, or not), see them in this way. Our drive to remain congruent with our identity is very, very powerful.

So next time you find yourself stressing out, or behaving in a way that you don't really understand or making repeated food or drink choices that are inconsistent with your knowledge base and how you want to take care of yourself, pause and ask yourself if you have perceived a loss or the risk that there may be a loss of love (safety).

Perhaps the perceived risk of loss was from an interaction you had with someone at the school gate, or at the office, or after a catch-up with a family member or friend. Or perhaps it's always there. It's just louder sometimes. Ask yourself if this stress you are feeling is showing you something that you are actually frightened of (a perceived loss of love due to how you think someone sees you, perhaps), and if so what it might be.

Through this enquiry, you'll likely come to see who you are trying to please and who you worry about when it comes to how they see you. And I hope in that moment you see how futile and unnecessary and, at times, damaging this is, because of the stress response it creates in you, the weight that it adds to your invisible load and the choices it leads you to make. When we scratch the itch that we are not enough, not acceptable, not worthy of love the way that we are, we do not usually make choices that support our health. You do not have to act a certain way for people to love and appreciate you. You just need to be you—your authentic self. And with the truth of all this, my hope is that you'll find a new way to live. With far less time spent with the stress response switched on and all the benefits that this brings.

How do you want to live?

Aligning your life with your values

I was backstage at a speaking job when two people in their early twenties rushed into the green room, excited to meet another of the speakers who was also in there. He was a highly successful businessman by Western standards, but he had a much bigger message to share with the world than just the secret to his success. The visitors asked him what he thought the next big thing would be, what aspect of technology perhaps, did he suggest they get involved in by starting their own business. His immediate response was that they'd asked the wrong question and by asking that question they were setting themselves up for aspects of their life to be miserable and overwhelming. He suggested that a better question to ask is 'how do I want to live?'

If he'd suggested to the enthusiastic pair that the next big thing was collective sourcing—offerings such as Airbnb, which had just launched at this stage—then if they set up a business like that, most of their days would be spent managing computer programmers, who may not value lively verbal communication, the way they clearly did. It might involve being indoors for all of the daylight hours and if their employees were night owls, some of the nights. And if they loved the sound of that then that would be a good business for them. But if none of that appealed to them, no matter how profitable that business could become, they wouldn't enjoy their life, and was that worth it?

So, a great question to ask yourself as you begin to unpack your invisible load is 'how do I want to live?' and then start taking steps—large or small—towards that. Many people wait to live in the way that they want to until something external to them shifts or they reach a certain age. This might (or not) be absolutely necessary for now, but it doesn't mean you can't take other more minor steps towards living the way you want to, until some of the bigger things can shift. Everyone lives thinking they have time, which you might. Or sadly not.

Your first response to the question 'how do I want to live?' might be 'I don't want to work', but we have to as money is required to live. So, this is not about reneging on basic essentials for life (unless you can go bush and live off the land). But it is very important to also ask yourself 'how much do I actually need?' from a monetary perspective as well as personal possessions, as insights gleaned in response to this question might also influence your choices and you end up working in paid employment for fewer hours than you currently do. It is good to keep researching whether the acquisition of things and doing more and more and more will bring you fulfilment.

The first time I asked myself how I wanted to live, one of the answers very close to the top of the list was 'I want to see more sunsets', as I am enamoured with watching light change. My work schedule at that stage was very full and I would regularly work well into the evening. So when I touched on how meaningful it would be to see the sunset each day, I decided that I may not be able to stop work for the evening at that time each day, but that I would close the lid of my laptop, take a break, watch the sunset and come back to my computer if I needed to. Some nights I went back but others I didn't. And that small step fostered a spaciousness in my brain that allowed me to see other aspects of my work and what was required in a new light. Additional changes gently followed. Your equivalent of watching the sunset might be a seemingly small step, but it can foster numerous other gradual shifts that lead to you living in a way that is more meaningful to you. And the impact of more meaning might just lead your pack to feel a little (or a lot) lighter.

When you ask yourself the question, 'how do I want to live?', have a pen and paper ready to capture what bubbles up. We sometimes fall into a way of life that we don't actually choose and then wake up years or decades later, wondering how it came to be this way. You might wonder how was it that when you met your partner, you came together

> WHEN YOU ASK YOURSELF THE QUESTION, 'HOW DO I WANT TO LIVE?', HAVE A PEN AND PAPER READY TO CAPTURE WHAT BUBBLES UP.

as equals. But somehow, you're the one who now carries the invisible load, as well as being the chief of remembering everything your household and family requires on top of your full-time paid work. And that this is not how you want to live. So you decide that delegation is going to be your focus over the coming months as you make some or all of the load visible, ask for help and share it or at least some of it.

You might decide you want to live with more energy so you start walking each day for half an hour to help with this. You might miss some people you love, and you start calling them once a week so they know you love and appreciate them. You might feel like what you do in your work doesn't make a big enough difference for your liking, so you decide to volunteer once a month and clear rubbish from your local beach or park.

Perhaps your heart breaks at the thought of elderly people having no one visit them in nursing homes so you decide to start visiting and before you know it, you're doing five manicures each Sunday morning—I know a lady who did and does exactly this. You might value not wasting things and you decide to give away the excesses you've accumulated gradually over time so you start with your linen cupboard and you deliver the extra sets of sheets and towels to your local women's refuge, so that the women and families who find safety and solace there have something to start over with.

Many people have lost leisure time—that space between work and sleep. Not that long ago, we tended to do eight hours of each—work, leisure, sleep. Now work has infiltrated into and encroached on our sleep and leisure time, making the latter non-existent for too many, undoubtedly adding to our invisible load. So, when you ask this question, perhaps your response involves exploring how you bring back more leisure time, with activities, adventures, pastimes or hobbies that light up your soul.

In response to 'how do I want to live?', you might do some budgets and financial calculations and work out how much you and your family actually need to live, add a small buffer and then just work to meet those needs so work doesn't own your life. Or perhaps you adore what you do and nothing about your work needs to change. Sometimes it's not WHAT we do that yearns to be changed but HOW we do it.

Having worked in health retreats for part of my life, I witnessed people who thrashed their bodies and minds and then tried to resuscitate these plus their souls for a week, before returning to life how it was before they arrived. As powerful and supportive as a week away in this type of environment is, it can be worthwhile to consider how might you live so that you incorporate aspects of self-care into your daily life, rather than you living in a way that leads you to burn out and need an ambulance or a complete life overhaul.

When you identify how you want to live, you may not be able to make some of the bigger changes for a decade. Yet by incorporating even tiny steps of gradual change, you might find that other aspects of your life shift in ways you can't currently predict. But, first, get clear within yourself.

What matters to you?

How do you want to live?

What do you want your days to look like?

mornings

daytime

evening

How much do you actually need? Think of this in the context of money, clothes, shoes, makeup and other life categories. Be specific.

What steps, large or small, can you take so that how you want to live becomes more aligned with how you actually live?

When did sadness become stress?

The fear of feeling

There is no question that sadness can be uncomfortable to feel. It can also feel overwhelming and all-consuming at times. Yet, I have been fascinated at the number of people who, when asked about scenarios where they have experienced stress, describe the loss of a loved one or a relationship separation. It prompted me to ponder: when did sadness become stress?

Do we try to cope with sadness by creating stress? Shifting our focus away from the depths of the emotional pain we start to feel but won't let ourselves fully feel—whatever is there—to drama or the consequences of the loss for ourselves and/or others. Or is it the tasks that often follow a loved one's death or a relationship ending that create the stress? Maybe it's a combination of both. Either way, most of us group it all together and call the whole lot 'stress', not really knowing how to feel sad so shifting our focus to the pile of tasks that now need doing and referring to all of that as 'stress' too.

Consider this. We feel grief and sadness at not being able to see a loved one who has passed or a partner who we now feel is off limits, or hold their hand, or hear their words of comfort or wisdom or laughter. While the emotion itself might rock us to our core, does the stress itself stem from the aftermath of the loss? Perhaps an elderly widower is now left living on his own and he requires assistance, or there may be challenging family dynamics as assets are disseminated or a will might be contested. These consequences of the person passing away might bring forth some stressful times. But the actual loss of someone you love—is that stress or is that grief? And if we're masking over these feelings with stress, where else are we doing this and what does this do to our invisible load?

In our society, we've never really been taught how to be with pain. In fact, many of us are taught that any 'negative' feeling is wrong.

We aren't taught this with actual words, but through observing how other people deal with these emotions when they come up, or how we ourselves are handled when these emotions come up for us. It happens when we're feeling sad and a parent, with the best of intentions, offers us ice cream to make us feel better. Or when we break up with someone we love, and our friends tell us there's plenty more fish in the sea. So, we might numb out with food, alcohol or other drugs, medications, brief sexual encounters or at times create drama or stresses to focus on, to divert our attention and focus away from our grief, or other strong, uncomfortable emotions. Of course, there may be real stress to deal with as well, but quite often we add to our own burden by not allowing ourselves to feel the sadness. So it persists as a rock in our pack longer than it would if we allowed ourself the full experience of the feeling and its unfolding in the first place. And one of the ways we avoid the sadness is by getting stressed.

WE'VE NEVER REALLY BEEN TAUGHT HOW TO BE WITH PAIN.

Perhaps the sadness that is present is due to a disappointed feeling you get sometimes when you examine how your life is. It might not feel fulfilling to you in its current state and you have moments where you wonder if this is all there is to it. You might feel like a slave to everyone else's needs (be aware of the potential, concurrent martyrdom in this, if so) and this is not the life you imagined for yourself. So instead of feeling how sad you really are about this, you blanket it with stress and constantly feel overwhelmed with life because ultimately it is your soul that is underwhelmed.

It also appears that, in many circles, saying you are stressed is more acceptable than saying you are sad. You might think that if you were to share your sadness with another, they might not be able to hold, handle or be present with what you are sharing. You don't want to be a burden or for others to think you are ungrateful for what you know is an amazing life, despite what you are going through, so you don't share a sadness that you are carrying and you've learnt to cover it over with days full of 'stress'. Yet being stressed stops us being vulnerable, while sadness fosters it. When you say you are stressed, does that feel hard or soft to you? It feels hard to me. Sadness, on

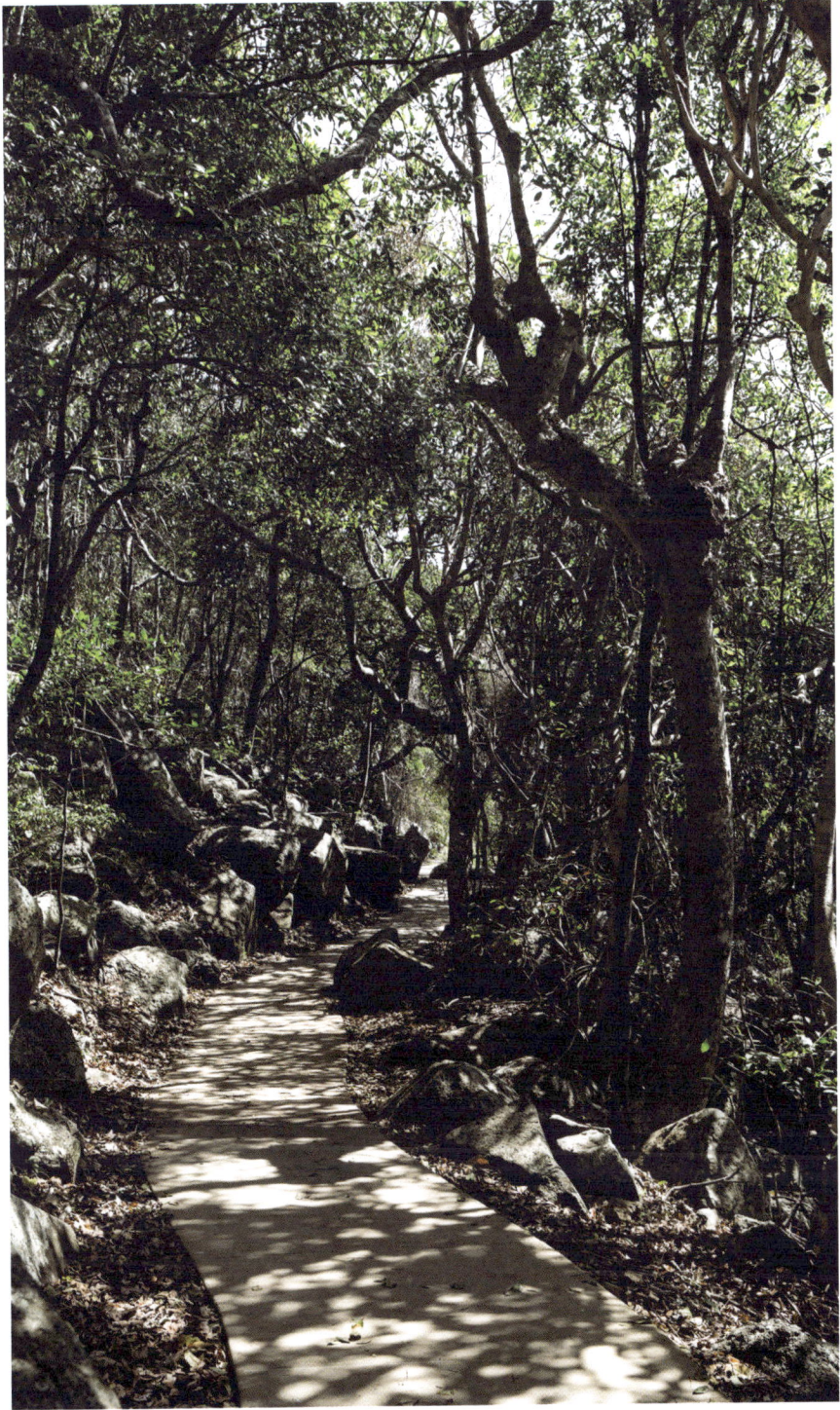

the other hand, requires us to first soften before it can be felt. Or sometimes we might be overcome with sadness and that, as ironic as it sounds, 'forces' us to soften. And many of us are so busy with our lives, so focused on getting on with it, and getting the tasks ticked off the list, that we don't create any space for ourselves to actually feel the sadness that is present, for whatever reasons—not just the loss of a loved one.

It is very feminine to soften and feel. And when you spend most of your days running everything—your life, the lives of others young and old, a business or a team, the household cooking and cleaning departments, the work and personal email inboxes—just to name a few, it is more masculine in nature.

> MANY OF US ARE SO BUSY WITH OUR LIVES, SO FOCUSED ON GETTING ON WITH IT, AND GETTING THE TASKS TICKED OFF THE LIST, THAT WE DON'T CREATE ANY SPACE FOR OURSELVES TO ACTUALLY FEEL THE SADNESS.

Of course, we as women are capable of all of this. We all have aspects of and can utilise the gifts of our masculine elements. It's just when we are unable, unwilling or it's unknown to us how essential it is to soften into our feminine as well each day that we can get lost in a bucket of overwhelming stress. When, really, if we let ourselves feel, and really teased out the emotions that are present, we'd see the range that is there.

There might be grief, sadness, despair and heartache that we've never acknowledged and unpacked. And once you go there, touch it and be with it, and open to it and feel it, it's less confronting than you likely anticipate it will be. Plus, it then transforms; some of your rocks get removed and some of the load falls away. At the absolute minimum you have a deeper level of compassion for yourself, which cannot help but then filter through to having more demonstrable compassion for others—and all of the physical, emotional, spiritual, soulful and community health benefits that brings.

The use of the word 'stressed' to describe the main emotion experienced by the death of a loved one or the ending of a significant, intimate relationship also made me wonder—have we all become inherently lazy with the language that we employ? We've not only stopped feeling but has our brain also become too busy to truly discern and describe what is really there? But think about it. When you know what is really there, whether you share it with anyone or not, it alters your responses.

How do you respond to sadness? Or disappointment, grief, despair, shame—even anger which often hides a deep fear or sadness? It can help to consider how you'd respond to someone else who came to you for support bearing these emotions, if it is difficult to be gentle with yourself. With caring and comforting actions is one way. But if you approach your difficult or painful emotions as stress, your internal response might involve the odd encouraging thought, something like 'you'll be right' or 'you can do this', but often there's a hardening involved too. An avoidance of feeling—almost out of fear that we'll crumble and get nothing done. 'For goodness sake, just get on with it' you might grumble to yourself or you brush it aside by thinking how worse off others in the world are and what right do you have to worry about anything? I know countless people, women in particular, who are so practised at shifting their focus from what's troubling them or what's behind their sadness, and going to gratitude when they feel 'stressed'—or upset or sad. When we do this, we never deal with the other emotions that are present or what is really bothering us and what we would benefit from changing! By all means be grateful—the world needs it—but become aware if you use it to sidestep what needs acting upon.

I cannot encourage you enough to allow yourself to truly feel what is there. You can always talk to a wise friend or seek professional support if it feels too frightening or confronting to go there on your own. You will soften and there are immense benefits that come from that. Like less muscle tension, more expansive breathing, more interior resources like blood flow, oxygen and nutrients available for healing and living—not to mention a deep peace and calm within that comes from acknowledging what truly is.

You must not be frightened
if a sadness rises up before you
larger than you have ever known,
casting its shadow over all you do.

You must think that something is
happening within you, and remember
that life has not forgotten you;
it holds you in its hand
and will not let you go.

– Rainer Maria Rilke

It also means less stress hormone production and the immensely beneficial ripple effects of this. Plus, it offers you the opportunity to be far more astute at discerning the emotions that are present in your landscape. This type of enquiry adds an incredible richness to our time on Earth and helps to foster a very deep caring for others in the process. If you think you don't have time for 'enquiry', I challenge you to try it while doing other tasks like watering the garden or renovating your bathroom, while you are making the bed or hanging out the washing, while you are driving home from work or before you check social media. It can be a relief to have a good sob in any of these scenarios, which is what might happen when you allow yourself to catch a glimpse of what is really there ... beyond the stress.

Consider Jamie Anderson's take on grief when she examined what was really there for her:

'Grief, I've learned, is really just love. It's all the love you want to give, but cannot. All that unspent love gathers up in the corners of your eyes, the lump in your throat, and in that hollow part of your chest. Grief is just love with no place to go.' [1]

Of course, none of what I'm saying is gospel. I'm simply offering you some new considerations about sadness, grief and other uncomfortable emotions we might avoid as well as the language patterns we use. Many people use the word 'stressed' to describe all kinds of emotions. I'm encouraging you to be specific. In doing so, all I'm hopeful of is that you and your body experience less stress and a deeply felt, lighter load.

---

* There is always help available. If ever your emotions become too overwhelming for you and you no longer feel safe, please contact Lifeline in New Zealand on 0800543354 or Lifeline in Australia on 131114.

Pain versus suffering

Inevitable or optional?

I remember, as a book-loving teenager, coming across the sentiment that suffering is not in the fact, but in the perception of the fact. In other words, pain is pain, but suffering is optional; we get to choose. Years later, one of the most profound books you will ever read, *Man's Search for Meaning* by Viktor Frankl, offered an even deeper perspective on this with his now famous words: *'Between stimulus and response there is a space. In that space is our power to choose our response. In our response lies our growth and our freedom.'* [1]

In writing about his experiences as a prisoner in Nazi concentration camps during World War II, with every member of his family having been killed, including his pregnant wife, Frankl shares how those holding him captive robbed him of his basic human dignity as well as anything that was of personal value to him. It was through this that he was able to discern that what could not be taken away from him was his choice about how to respond to the trauma and degradation of these circumstances. To be able to retain such a high level of psychological autonomy in the most horrendous of situations offers us an extraordinary example of the power of personal choice, grace under immense duress and the Serenity Prayer in action (coming up on page 243). [2]

We too can choose how we respond to everything. You can make a conscious choice to own that minuscule space between the stimulus—whatever is said or done 'to' you—and your response to that. This is not to suggest that you don't recognise what is there: devastation, grief, shame, anxiety, loneliness—whatever the emotions are. Embracing your emotions allows you to own them, rather than them owning you. By altering our thinking and how we think about our thinking, we can

EMBRACING YOUR EMOTIONS ALLOWS YOU TO OWN THEM, RATHER THAN THEM OWNING YOU.

adjust our emotional responses and the extent to which we suffer, or not. Our thoughts, not what happens, literally have the capacity to make us miserable. Or not. Let's distinguish a little further between pain and suffering.

When you feel physical pain, there are distinct biological and psychological mechanisms at work. Biologically, signals are communicated via the nervous system to alert you to something not being right. This can save our life obviously if we place our hand too close to an open flame. However, we might also take it further with our thinking. In our heads we interpret and give meaning to these biological signals and anything at all that we give meaning to is adulterated. It is tainted. It is not what it is, but rather filtered through the beliefs that we have, most of which, until we do inner work, are unknown to us. Some beliefs enhance the quality of our lives, some take away from it. If you have a belief that pain is a way you get attention, you will likely enjoy aspects of it—not the pain itself but what it brings you. If your beliefs about pain run more along the lines of it helping to draw your attention to changes you need to consider making with how you eat, drink, move, think, breathe or perceive, you'll see it as an opportunity to learn and grow. Suffering, therefore, is an outcome from our emotional responses to the pain. Pain is inevitable whereas suffering is not, because the suffering occurs as a result of our thinking, our perceptions and the meanings we give things.

A common one I've witnessed that only leads to suffering is 'poor me', closely followed by 'this isn't fair'. 'Poor me' is the ultimate statement of victim mentality—you feel sorry for yourself relentlessly, not momentarily. It is very difficult for your biochemistry or your psychology to support you getting well if this is a mantra you tend to knowingly or unknowingly recite.

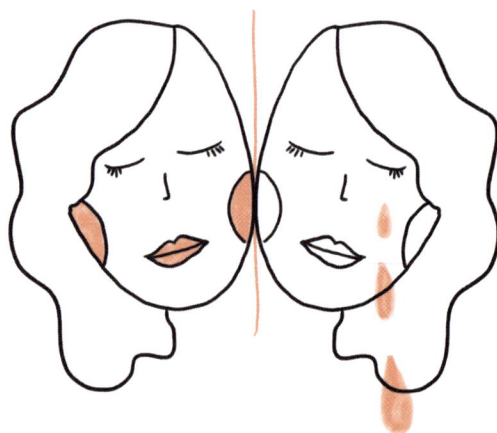

Imagine you go through a relationship break-up. Through your (now former) relationship, you and your (now ex) partner have had a consistent friendship circle that you've socialised with together. Now that you've broken up, you want your (joint) friends to support you and you don't feel comfortable with them maintaining a relationship with your ex. But they do. And this really pushes your buttons. You begin to notice all the ways that (you perceive) they now exclude you from certain events while they seemingly continue to make plans with your ex. This makes you feel as if your friends like your ex more than they like you. It feels like no one has your back, that no one supports you, that you're entirely on your own. So you project all of your hurt and disappointment at your ex and blame them for not being considerate of your feelings. You feel like none of this is fair— that no one cares or understands how you're feeling. This way of thinking and meaning making spirals you into a whirlpool of unnecessary suffering.

Can you see how you choose meanings rather than living from how things actually are? Given the same pain, someone else might not create any meanings and they will literally just deal with what is in front of them. Or they may think about how everyone will be experiencing a level of anguish about this break-up and that everyone needs time to adjust and true friends find their way home together. Or perhaps the thinking would be more along the lines of there is enough love to go around and no one has to miss out here. With a physical illness, some people go to 'poor me' and repeat to themselves how it isn't fair that this is what's happening and live in their suffering, likely prolonging the illness as a result. Others faced with the same illness might think that that was one way to slow them down and that their body is telling them that they need to rest more or that they've been given the space to reassess their life. Or they might think 'if this is happening for me, rather than to me, what is the gift in this?'

> YOU CAN CHOOSE TO DISTINGUISH BETWEEN PAIN AND SUFFERING. THE FORMER IS INEVITABLE WHILE THE LATTER IS OPTIONAL.

I'm not for one second suggesting this is easy—but it is possible. It takes courage, and a desire to lead a life that might be different from how it is now. It also takes presence and an awareness of HOW you think, not subjects we are taught in school. You can choose to distinguish between pain and suffering. The former is inevitable while the latter is optional.

Having worked with people who experience chronic pain, they can end up in a nasty vicious cycle where pain (understandably) drives lousy thoughts and self-denigration. This leads to suffering which elevates stress hormone production from the adrenal glands, stimulates the sympathetic nervous system and increases muscle tension. These signals tend to amplify pain which triggers more stress hormones and tension to be produced. [3] Experienced psychologists can support a patient to modify their suffering through understanding the biological pathways of pain and helping them to find new ways to respond to pain. It is such a gift to the patient when they become aware that they can change their responses. It doesn't necessarily mean the pain isn't felt. It is, however, the response that alters.

Physical pain aside, so much of our overwhelm and the weight of our invisible load stems from suffering and most of us have never been taught, nor have we paused to consider, how we might choose a different road or a different way of thinking. Because we see the world through the lenses of our beliefs, we don't often even realise that there is another way to think or see aspects of our life. Yet when you know how you think, you can acknowledge how you feel and, in doing this, begin to change how you feel.

As you become more responsible for your responses, be patient with yourself. Remember that how you have been responding up until now has likely been your pattern, your way, for all but about a couple of years at the very beginning of your life. So, we might still run the responses of old, but because we now know better, we don't stay in that place for long. We return to the truth, which is that we get to choose how we respond. Something might happen and you run the old response wiring. Just notice that and nod knowingly in recognition of what you just did. Then return to the moment and pause to consider your response.

Sure, it takes practice and awareness, yet what's on offer is a whole lot of freedom and peace even though what you have to (I prefer 'get to') do each day hasn't changed. But your perspective has. And this shift can go a long way to reducing your invisible load.

We owe a great deal to Viktor Frankl for what he shared, for it is so very true that what lies between the stimulus and our response is every ounce of our growth and freedom. Which is why I wholeheartedly believe that nothing happens to us, it all happens FOR us—if we choose to respond in that way.

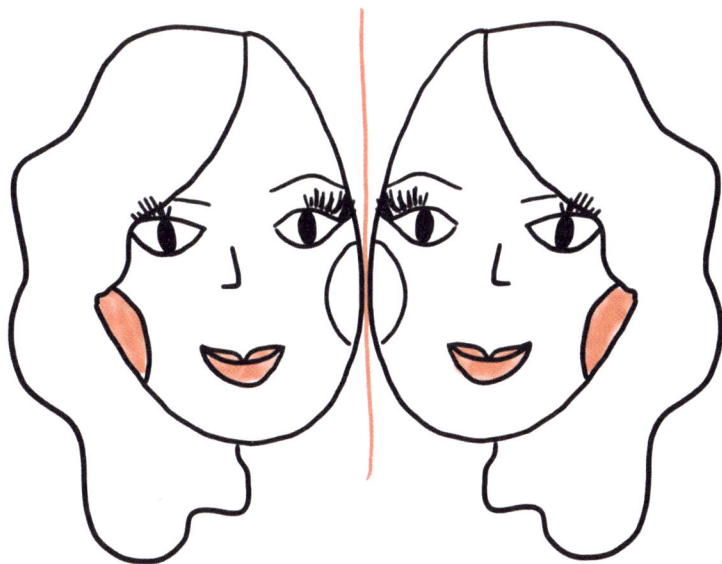

Forget the
mistake.

Remember
the lesson.

ANON

THE GLOBAL LOCAL ISSUE

a beauty undone

the astringent of the orange

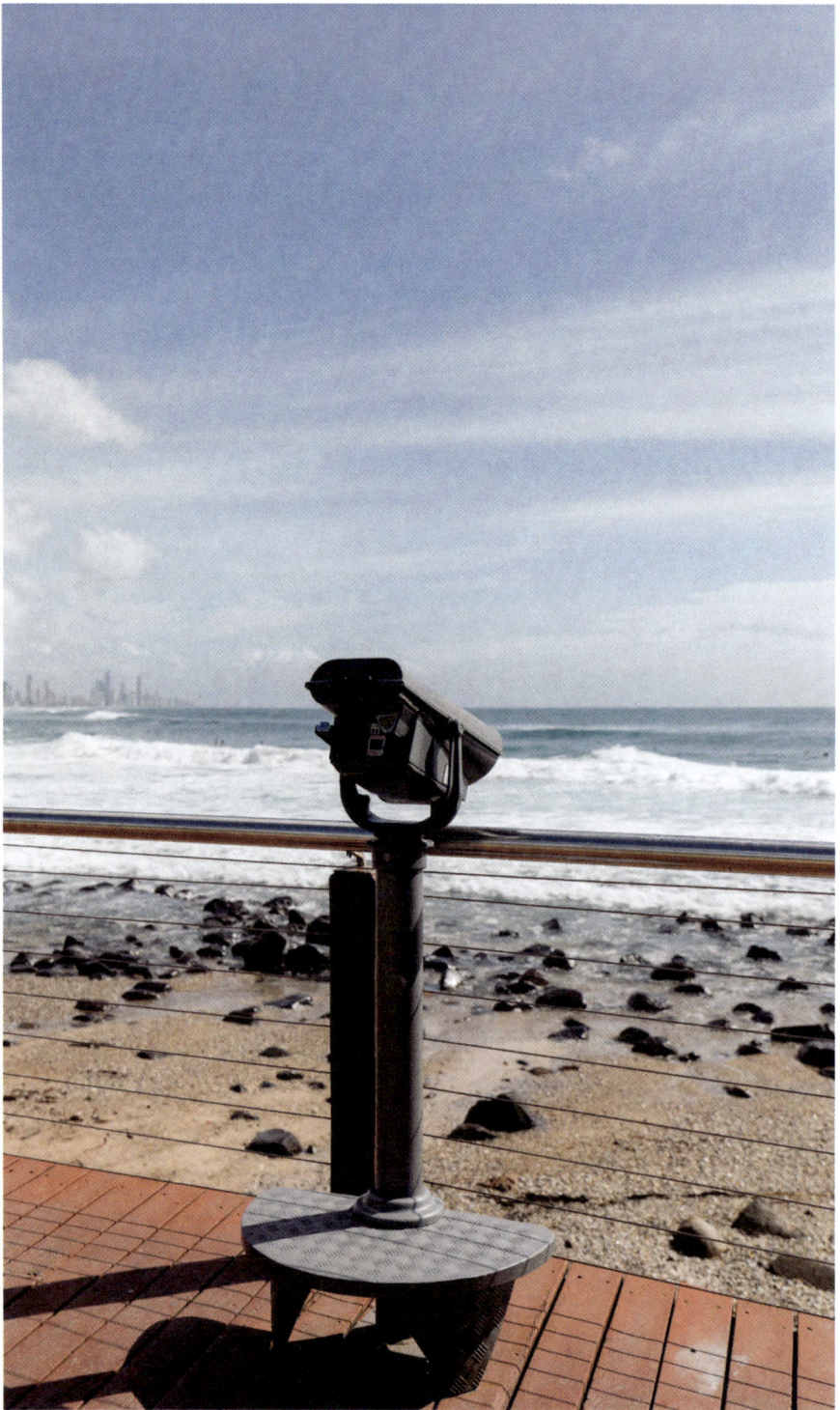

How do you think?

Getting to the heart of your stress

When exploring overwhelm and the invisible load, I wanted to dig in deep, to peer behind the veil that clouds our clarity when it comes to what stress really is for us. Rather than simply encourage you to 'breathe diaphragmatically to lower stress hormones' and 'take some adaptogenic medicinal herbs like withania (ashwagandha)'—which are both very useful and can make a significant difference—I felt it was time to do what we can to not make the stress hormones in the first place. Turn off the tap rather than trying endlessly to fill a bath tub without the plug being in.

When it comes to stress, there are commonalities in the basis of our stress but also scenarios that are highly individual. To examine what's truly at the heart of our stress, instead of scrutinising WHAT stresses us out, we need to examine HOW we actually think. So, I have set out to share with you the best way I can currently explain my take on HOW we, as humans, think and see the world and ourselves. I want to help you to see how you think because when you know how you think, you can change how you feel. This is integral to unpacking your own backpack of stress and lightening your load. Let's take a step back through your life to explore the ways in which thoughts and beliefs develop.

OUR FIRST FEARS

Every human's greatest fear is that they won't be loved. It's not always easy to see this initially, but you'll often find it when you examine where you don't feel like you are enough—smart enough, tall enough, pretty enough, kind enough, patient enough, successful enough—just not good enough the way that you are. The reason we fear not being loved is not some artificial construct dreamt up by modern psychologists. This fear is hard-wired into us at birth because someone has to attend to our needs as a little human so we can survive. Someone has to provide us with food, clothing and shelter as we cannot obtain these for ourselves and, without them, when we are young, we will die. Other animals can forage and survive on their own, right from birth. And as I mentioned on page 172, eventually we link the attention and response to our needs by a parent or carer to love. That's how love gets its super potent connection to survival. It is wired into the ANS.

Yet, as an adult, we know that a life with love in it is soul-nourishing and delicious, but we can survive without it, as we can meet our own basic needs. Yet most of us live our whole lives as if love is essential to our survival. And until you examine it, the fear of a loss of love will literally run your life, all of your choices and be at the heart of your stress.

YOUR YOUNG BRAIN

As young humans, from an emotional maturation perspective we are egocentric. All that means is that you believe you are the centre of the universe and that everyone in your world is the way they are because of you. So, when they are happy, a part of your brain (which I'll explain in a moment) links it to whatever you've just done. For example, if you're four years old and you've just smashed out a finger painting and you unknowingly notice your mum is smiling and playful, your brain, unbeknown to you, links how she is to what you've just done. If this occurs enough times, an artist will be born.

If you're four and you love dress-ups and have had three outfit changes and thrown on a splash of Mum's lippy before brekkie most days of the week (I bet Mum is still in her pyjamas!), and Mum constantly cracks up at you and looks delighted, a fashion stylist might be born. When you examine aspects of your personality as an adult from this viewpoint, you can start to see where much of it originated.

However, the same is true when those you rely on to help you survive in those early years are in a lousy place. They might be quiet and withdrawn, or verbally loud, or slam fists on tables as they are communicating. Without knowing it, as a child with the level of emotional maturation you are capable of at this stage, your brain cannot see into their world and see that they are a product of their joys and their challenges up until this point in time. You cannot see that they had a challenging day at work or that an unexpected bill has just landed in the letterbox and your parent doesn't know

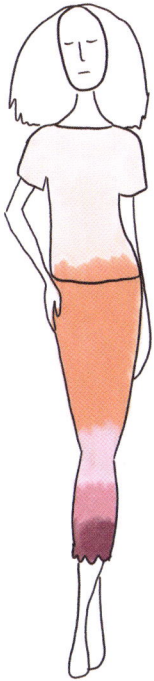

Where have you been?

Finding yourself is not
really how it works.

You aren't a ten-dollar bill in last
winter's coat pocket.

You are also not lost.

Your true self is right there, buried
under cultural conditioning, other
people's opinions, and inaccurate
conclusions you drew as a kid that
became your beliefs about
who you are.

'Finding yourself' is actually
returning to yourself.
An unlearning, an excavation, a
remembering who you were before
the world got its hands on you.

EMILY MCDOWELL[1]

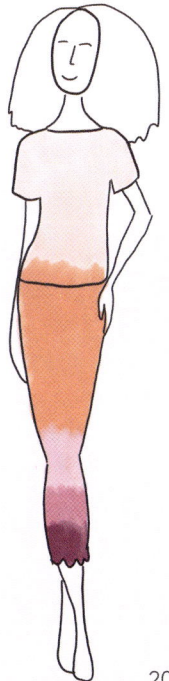

I've always been right here!

where they will get the money from to pay it. At this stage in your development, your brain will not let you see their 'flaws' or understand that there are things that ignite emotional responses in adults that have nothing to do with you. If you were to catch a glimpse of that, you might run away, which would likely put your survival at risk, trying to fend for yourself at such a young age.

Whenever there is confusion—you don't understand why Dad usually plays with you when he comes home from work, but for the past three days, he hasn't done this, he's barely spoken to you—your brain will try to make sense of what's happening in an attempt to return your biochemistry and psychology back to homeostasis (to safety). Your dad may have been made redundant and he's internalising his stress, worrying about how he is going to pay for your education. But you don't know this. All you experience is that his behaviour has changed. And because you are four, your brain has zero other options to explain what's going on, other than for you to create a belief in your own deficiency. You're not even at school yet and you now believe there is something wrong with you.

> YOU'RE NOT EVEN AT SCHOOL YET AND YOU NOW BELIEVE THERE IS SOMETHING WRONG WITH YOU.

However, you don't know you now have this belief. You don't sit there and actively choose it, rolling your eyes to yourself about how dysfunctional it might make your life by the time you are 45! Nope. That's not how we humans roll. You absorb the beliefs in response to what is occurring, as a part of your brain tries to make sense of your environment. You're egocentric at this stage, remember? You make it about you. When you are young you don't have a choice in that. You can't make it about your parents or carer at such an early phase in your emotional development. I'm not talking about overt abuse here. Just everyday interactions. Yet even when a child is undeniably abused by their parents, the child doesn't tend to stop loving them. The child more often stops loving themselves.

How does our brain come to the conclusion that we must not be worthy of being loved when we are still so innocent? It's heartbreaking when you consider it that way, isn't it? Yet because there is not a human who escapes this, no matter how calm or chaotic it is for them growing up, there must be an evolutionary purpose to it, surely? We'll go digging into that in a moment.

BEING AND DOING

When you were two years old, what did you have to do to be loved? Nothing. You just had to exist. However, once you have a belief that silently informs you (beliefs are like lenses or filters that you unknowingly look through—more on this in a moment) that you have to be a certain way, look a particular way, never be something else, now you BELIEVE that you have to DO certain things to be loved. I call it the schism. Because up until then you just existed. It is the inaugural shift from a human being to a human doing. It's the beginning of the invisible load.

We unknowingly believe we have half a chance of regaining the love we perceive we have lost—a feeling of safety that we now crave in every cell of our body, the nervous system in particular—if we DO certain things in a certain way: get good grades, clean up after ourselves, put others' needs ahead of our own, always be kind, never be selfish… Or perhaps perceived rewards or favourability when you were growing up were more along the lines of having to keep secrets, stay quiet, and pretend that everything at home was happy families, to keep a parent on side.

Yet goodness also stems from these actions and traits. If you are kind and thoughtful, you tend to have true friends because you are a true friend. You also tend to foster a great sense of community through your kind and sharing ways. If you are good at keeping secrets, you will likely be a trustworthy friend, rather than gossiping about other people's stories. Being quiet often makes you a very good listener. The world NEEDS all of this! So beautiful things can come from your false belief about who you have to be to be loved.

So, a purpose to the original wound? It makes us contribute and it fosters our growth. It drives us to do things, to take action. In other words, if all our needs were always met, would we actually do anything? I cannot answer that because at this stage in our evolution, no one avoids this path. Even when it is calm in your childhood home and there is tenderness

and care and presence and no raised voices (which typically signal alarm to the nervous systems around you, even if you're just venting frustrations about a particular political situation, for example), there will be a moment when something is said, when a part of your brain hears what is said and creates a meaning (unbeknown to you) that there has been a loss of the certainty of love.

Let's say you missed the school bus one afternoon. You start walking home and it's a long way. Your worried mum drives to find you and after a period of silence while she calms down from the distress she's just been through (and she's never been silent with you before), the first words she utters are 'you've really disappointed me'. Remember you believe, via your nervous system and senses, that you rely on this person for survival. And this person, who is vital, essential to you staying alive, no longer holds you in high esteem (none of which you think consciously). A part of your brain perceives there has been a loss of love. Yet Mum just said what she said as she is opening up a conversation to ensure your future safety. She didn't set out to hurt you in any way. Precisely the opposite in fact. And at the end of the conversation, a different part of your brain from the one that perceived the loss of love initially in an instant might have worked out that she said all of that because she cares. But your hidden initial response to this situation has, unknowingly to you, now given you a belief that you must never let anyone down.

> WHEN YOU WERE TWO YEARS OLD, WHAT DID YOU HAVE TO DO TO BE LOVED? NOTHING. YOU JUST HAD TO EXIST.

Because if you do go letting people down, it leads to the ultimate pain—the (perceived) loss of love from someone who you rely on to survive. And you will do ANYTHING to avoid feeling like this, including sacrifice your own health through how you live.

Or take the teenage boy whose dad has struggled with debilitating depression across the years. Dad's challenges could lead him to withdraw and stay in bed for days at a time and then go through periods where he would repeatedly explode in a rage. A child in that environment might start taking drugs in an attempt to numb the pain that stems from unconsciously deciding that he mustn't be enough for his dad to want to do what he perceives other dads do with their sons. He can't truly perceive of his father's pain and what that is like for him. Or, maybe, the teenager's brain takes a different path and decides that if he is always 'good', always well behaved, 'Dad values money and wealth so I'll work myself into the ground at school to get the highest grades so I can get a fantastic job and then he'll be proud of me and that will surely help Dad to be happier'. Not that that rationale is conscious. Same stimulus (Dad's challenges). Different response (numbing pain with drugs or feeling like your life (and the quality of Dad's) depends on you working obscenely hard). Sadly, one will be frowned upon and one will be rewarded in this Western world of ours. But it all stems from the same pain.**

And that's what I mean that it doesn't matter how calm or chaotic it was at home while you were growing up. Just through everyday interactions, there is a part of our brain that has an instantaneous response to situations we are a part of and if we don't know that this has occurred—through learning HOW we think—or that we have the ability to analyse and reassess this silent but rapid-fire response, it will run your life and you will have no idea why you feel so stressed all the time. You'll just think it's work and the mortgage and the kids, because those are the things you can see.

**If you have displayed strong emotions in front of a child or shared with them any thoughts or feelings of despair and are now deeply upset, please do not feel guilty. Everyone does their best. No one sets out to hurt a child, including you. They just express their unresolved pain and there is unfortunately sometimes collateral damage. I am simply offering examples of scenarios to show how beliefs become established in all of us in childhood, which will also have occurred for you, so please bring compassion to yourself. Please seek support if you feel triggered by what you have just read or desire new ways to deal with your pain.

WHO MUST I BE?

When the schism occurs, you don't even know that a part of your young-self brain has asked the question: 'Who must I be for them to treat me this way? These people who I hero-worship, whose APPROVAL, attention, admiration and love that I don't just want but that I NEED (to survive according to your nervous system)—who must I be for them to treat me this way? What must be wrong with me for this to be happening?' But just like that, unbeknown to you, a belief forms about WHO YOU ARE, as this is the only way you can make sense of your environment. 'Yep, there's something wrong with me and I will now set about proving myself right regularly' (more on why you see it this way in a moment), 'plus I'll set about proving to them that I am good enough and that I am actually worth loving'.

And every choice you then make stems from you wanting to earn back their approval (love) that you think you've lost. Your work ethic? Where did that come from? Your unrelenting kindness—you feel like you have no option than to turn up as a ray of sunshine in everyone else's life? Your desire to always be seen as perfect and ALL of the things you do in an attempt to be seen in this way? The way you rush from task to task and overfill your days, when you wish you wouldn't? Why? And until you examine this, your pursuit of their approval will never end. And you will unknowingly live as if whatever you do, and however you are, will never be enough.

As adults, many people make some sort of peace with major or minor challenges they had with those who raised them by understanding that they did the best they could with the resources —including knowledge—that they had access to and a recognition that they had much pain of their own. We may (or not) forgive entirely but we can understand on a conscious level. But what about the system of thought that came up with the beliefs? That quick as a flash decided, unknowingly to you, that you mustn't be worthy of their love, that there must be something wrong with you, that you aren't good enough. What about that part? That's not the same thought system that reasons as an adult that they did their best. And here's our challenge in our current evolutionary state: these two thought systems don't really talk to each other.

Be you

So even though by now, as an adult, you likely know that they both love/d you in their own way, there will be one of them whose love you wanted more. Perhaps one was consistent in how they loved you, he/she was unwavering in his/her support of you and loved you unconditionally. So, because you never had to question his/her love, it was the other parent's love you craved. Or perhaps they were both lousy. Whose love did you want most? Or maybe they were both present and attentive and from a young age your needs were met and your nervous system didn't get rattled until high school and so you had 12 years of 'safety'—there will still be one whose love you craved the most. It can be incredibly insightful to work out who this was and what you perceived you had to do to be loved and also what you could never do for this person in an attempt to gain certainty of their love for you. How did you have to BE for this person? What did you have to DO? Who could you never be and what could you never do? I encourage you to really examine this and answer those questions.

BELIEFS AND A FILTERED VIEW

Once we have a belief it changes how we look out upon the world. It is as if you've popped on a pair of tinted glasses and now all you see is filtered through a lens. The same filters also cover your ears so that anything you hear has also altered from how you heard things before the belief formed. So now you don't hear what someone says, instead you hear what you perceive they meant. Your beliefs determine how you see and experience EVERYTHING and they drive your behaviour and choices.

There is a part of your brain called the reticular activating system (RAS) that goes looking for evidence of your beliefs. This system is behind what is known as 'confirmation bias': once a belief is in place, we screen what we see and hear in a tainted way that ensures our beliefs are 'proven' correct. The RAS finds what you are looking for— if you have a belief that love is dangerous and something that can only ever hurt you, when someone you love dies suddenly your brain thinks 'see, it isn't safe to love'. Whereas someone else will think 'gosh, I'd better make the most of every day. You never know when it might all be over'. But because you have no idea that there's another way to respond, other than the way that you have responded, you can't even see that your response to the stimulus is of your own making, based on beliefs you have that you aren't aware of, and that you chose it. Remember Viktor Frankl's insightful words (see page 197)?

When you want to buy a new car you suddenly see the model you like everywhere, don't you? That's the RAS at work, finding what you have primed your brain to find. And exactly the same thing happens with your beliefs. You unknowingly look for evidence of them everywhere. So, if you believe you aren't good enough or that you are a failure, everything you see and hear will be filtered through this belief, convincing you of its truth and you will miss all of the examples of how this is not true.

None of this is to pass judgement on how anyone responds to anything. You respond based on your life conditions up until this point, and as I said earlier, no one has a clue what it is like to be you. I'm simply suggesting that you examine the responses you choose. For if they bring you joy (and many of them will), and a functional life that is meaningful to you, then excellent. But if they bring you undone, not occasionally, but regularly, and you feel overwhelmed and permanently stressed, then conjure some curiosity and go digging in here. Start to notice your responses as they will start to show you your beliefs.

Beliefs are slippery to find because they are tied up in language patterns. And you can't hear your beliefs when you say them because, for you, they aren't beliefs, they are reality. When brothers grow up with a dysfunctional alcoholic father and one brother also becomes a dysfunctional alcoholic and the other one doesn't, the former will say he is the way he is because of his father. And the latter man will say the same. Stimulus. Response. And the response stems from beliefs.

It is through the filters created by our beliefs that we stop dealing with what actually occurs and instead we create meanings about what occurs. We believe something to be true (we're not pretty enough) and then something happens (someone we are sweet on doesn't text us back) and we create a meaning about it (we're single because we aren't pretty enough). Your brain rapidly merges the two—the 'what happens' and the 'meaning'—but you can't see that your brain has done this. So, all you take forward into your future

is the meaning you created—that you literally made up—and your beliefs fostered the meaning you made. And then you live as if the meaning is true. In fact, you can't even see that you've made a meaning. You think the meaning is what happened. And from the quality of these meanings stems the greatest of times and the worst of times. And with the latter, so much stress for you to carry.

EGOCENTRIC?

Too many adults have not emotionally outgrown the egocentrism of their childhood level of maturation. And that's partly because the thought system that makes everything about ourselves, rather than instantaneously considering what might be going on for the other person, still does this, trying to keep you safe. It doesn't mean to be self-focused, but it was made that way to look after you for the first 200 or so pages of the *Homo sapiens* evolution book (referencing the evolutionary time concept on page 36). Yet another thought system knows better. However, that won't stop you worrying that you've upset a colleague when he usually stops in the doorway of your office for a chat each morning on his way back from the tea room and then one morning you see him walk straight past. In that moment, your brain runs an emotional response pattern akin to the one it ran this morning when the barista was seemingly 'weird' with you at your local café and the one you'll run this afternoon when your friend still hasn't responded to your request to catch up over the weekend, days later.

Silently inside, our 'protective' mechanism makes it all about us. It can take hours or days or even weeks before you wonder what might have been going on for the other person, when you catch a glimpse of an alternative to what you came up with in the moment when these things initially happened. Plus, between the day when you had these three experiences, and now when you are awakening to the truth—that they had things on their mind, that they were drowning in work, that they read your message at a busy period in their day and just forgot about it and then got caught up with the family routine— how have you treated yourself? With highly nourishing food choices and water as your main drink? Unlikely.

You will continue with whatever strategies you've concocted over the years to escape from your (emotional) pain, behaviour you don't feel you can control or stop, or choices where you judge yourself for having no willpower. That's what you'll do. Even though you know better and you wish you wouldn't. But you still do. And you do it so that you don't have to feel, truly FEEL, what a thought system has found 'more evidence for'—that you are… Fill in the blank with the belief. That you are not good enough, that you are not cool enough, that you are not attractive enough, that you are a failure or a fraud, that you always let others down—all of them beliefs that this same thought system MADE UP a long time ago to try to help you feel safe in your environment. And it is where the majority—if not all—of your stress and overwhelm come from.

So many of our challenges can be found in what we say after a comma. 'I ate too many biscuits, therefore I am hopeless, pathetic and have no willpower.' After the comma is the judgement and it's the judgement that undoes you. It's the harsh verdict you place upon yourself after taking an action (eating too many biscuits) that leads you to eat more biscuits or engage with other behaviours and thoughts that hurt you. It's also an inaccurate examination of what happened. You might have eaten too many biscuits because you were hungry, as you didn't eat any carbs for lunch. Or perhaps you ate too many biscuits because you were in a meeting at work prior to the biscuit session, and although you put on a brave face, something someone in the meeting said hurt your feelings. And after the comma is your patterned, instantaneous, initially hidden response that you believe to be the truth. But you've made the whole thing up. Remember childhood and making sense of our environment?

So, in the pause of breath in a sentence when you want to add a comma, enquire within about whether a full stop would serve you better in that moment. Examine what you wanted to say after a comma and you'll start to see some of your beliefs, enabling you to begin to unpack them and return to the Truth. If you use the full stop in your sentence (I ate too many biscuits.), next, try asking 'I wonder what led me to do that?' and with

SO, ALL YOU TAKE FORWARD INTO YOUR FUTURE IS THE MEANING YOU CREATED– THAT YOU LITERALLY MADE UP–AND YOUR BELIEFS FOSTERED THE MEANING YOU MADE.

the curiosity those words evoke, you will open to new information, rather than closing down and becoming blind to insight because of harsh self-judgement. The judgement doesn't just stop you from knowing the Truth, it leads you to keep living as if the stories you made up about yourself are real and with the stress and the load that those patterns and choices can induce.

THE THOUGHT SYSTEMS

Having looked at beliefs and meanings and where our behaviours and choices come from, I want to peel back another layer and examine how our systems of thought function and how, when unchecked, they can lead us to lousy self-esteem, subsequent poor quality lifestyle choices, and living life overwhelmed with our heavy invisible load. Let's explore HOW we think.

On page 35, I raised the concept of our two brains—essentially, two systems of thought. Technically, I prefer to refer to them as thought systems but this can lead to confusion. So, to assist, we could name them with a whole range of comparative names:

Thought System 1	Thought System 2
Brain 1	Brain 2
Old Brain	New Brain
Feeling	Reason
Super-speed	Slow-poke
Hare	Tortoise

For ease of understanding, I'll stick with Old Brain and New Brain and use these interchangeably with Feeling and Reason.

Feeling (Old Brain): works without our conscious awareness, is fast as lightning and the source of snap judgements that we experience as a hunch or intuition or as emotions like fear, worry or unease. A decision that comes from Feeling is hard or impossible to explain in words. You have no idea why you feel the way you do, you just do. [2] And you may not even realise when this thought system has generated a feeling, or be able to name it.

Reason (New Brain): works slowly, examines evidence, calculates and considers. When Reason makes a decision, it is easy to put into words and explain it. [2]

The Old Brain works as rapidly as it does because it uses built-in rules of thumb and automatic settings [2] created across the entirety of the evolution of our species. One such rule is that if examples of things can be recalled easily, we have a setting that has helped us survive that says that such things must be common. [2] In this day and age, this may or may not be true. Let's say you don't travel for work often and if you do, you drive. But next week you are flying somewhere. Remember your hypothalamus—the region where your endocrine and nervous systems meet—constantly repeats 'am I safe?' and is forever assessing risks. As you unconsciously pose this question to yourself, you try to retrieve examples of plane crashes or airport safety challenges that you might have heard about. If your brain can rapidly come up with examples, Old Brain (Feeling) will set off the alarm that the risk is high, telling you to be frightened. So you will be. But you won't know why because Old Brain operates without our conscious awareness. All you'll notice is that you now feel uneasy about your trip next week, but you'd find it difficult to truly explain why you feel this way. [2] So, Old Brain is brilliant and it is also flawed. Brilliant because it uses simple rules of thumb that foster an instantaneous assessment of a situation, which solidifies a judgement—just what you need when walking home late at night on your own when you don't have the latest crime stats available for analysis. But it is also flawed because the same rules of thumb can spawn irrational conclusions. [2]

When someone you know who you see at the supermarket walks past and doesn't speak to you, you don't consciously rationalise the experience. You might later, but initially Old Brain has a knee-jerk, instantaneous response to what you experience—fear. Fear you've let her down, fear she no longer likes you, fear your children have had a scuffle at school and you're now ostracised for being a lousy parent... You don't consciously think any of this through though. You're not even aware you've perceived this. You might notice that before you went to the supermarket life was fine—not tremendously gleeful but not dreadful either. It was fine. And now you feel anything but fine. You're worrying about what you've done to Mrs Supermarket and then your thoughts gain momentum and you start thinking about other people who you think probably don't like you or you worry you've

Choose your playlist

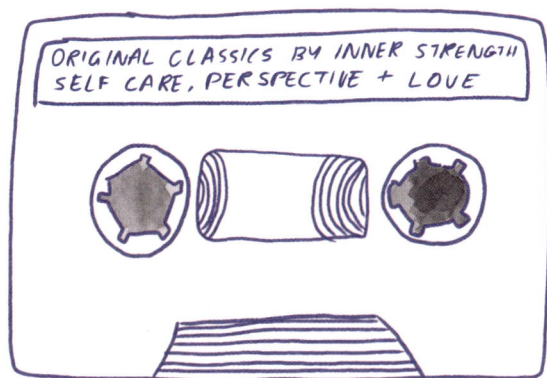

FEATURING TRACKS OF SELF LOATHING.
GUILT. JEALOUSY + YOUR INNER FEARS

ORIGINAL CLASSICS BY INNER STRENGTH
SELF CARE, PERSPECTIVE + LOVE

offended. And then you go even lower in your thoughts and tell yourself you're not a worthwhile person and then you flip from the self-denigration and get momentarily pious and from your pulpit to the far reaches of your mind you exclaim you'd never treat anyone that way, how dare she ignore you! And then you use whatever your numbing mechanism is to blunt, divert and obfuscate this emotional turmoil. When all that's happened is Mrs Supermarket probably didn't see you as she has a huge amount on her mind and was focused on ensuring she didn't forget the gingernuts. But you've gone and done a right number on yourself (which, if you did this in response to this scenario, you likely do a version of this multiple times, most days) and the ripple effect of this invisible load might impact what you eat and drink, whether you move (exercise), how you think, the way you breathe (hello stress hormone production) and perceive for the rest of the day/night. If you're lucky.

Or the ripple might last for weeks or months across which time you've taken lousy care of yourself. Not because you don't know better. But because Feeling (Old Brain) runs your show. And you believe yourself. You don't even know you can bring Reason (New Brain) in and make some rational, adult (rather than childhood, egocentric) assessments.

And so much of our emotional overwhelm stems from what Feeling generates and what Reason fails to examine.

What would Reason (New Brain) do? It will still be influenced by your beliefs about who you are, of course (the ones you've made up). But Reason will allow you to bring awareness and apply conscious, exploratory thinking to the situation. You might not even initially see that your change in behaviour and mood began after that interaction. But that's how you find it: you look for the moment just before you felt or behaved differently. What did you think or perceive? Up until then, you might have been taking good care of your food choices, for example, and then seemingly out of nowhere, you binged, or ate too much ice cream or a packet of lollies. Even though on the surface it might look like nothing has changed, something has. Feeling (Old Brain) concocted something—with your best interests at heart. It's just that Old Brain does well navigating your life when you've gathered and foraged all day and are spending your evenings around a camp fire. She's dazed and confused and cannot comprehend a world where she finds herself among the bright lights of the supermarket.

The Feeling system (Old Brain) has always kept us safe. We've never questioned her. Reason (New Brain) doesn't even know it needs to check in with what Feeling has come up with to assess its accuracy. If your friend Claire hasn't called you for three weeks when you usually hear from her at least once a week, Feeling will usually send you UNKNOWINGLY off on an emotional goose chase because Feeling will decide it's because there is a strong chance, a risk, that she no longer likes you. If she doesn't like you, it means she no longer cares for you, which Feeling links to protection and safety (set up in all humans as babies; wired into the ANS) so Feeling has you, silently and unconsciously, deeply fearful. And we'll label this as stressed and chalk up not hearing from Claire as just another thing on our list that's not right in our world. You might assess the situation in time and come up with the possibility that Claire might just be busy or overwhelmed herself (prompting you to reach out to her and check in). But until Reason (New Brain) examines what Feeling (Old Brain) decided, you might just not feel like your usual chirpy self, or you feel tired for reasons you can't explain, or you'll do what many do which is partake in food and beverage behaviours that hurt them and that they don't understand. You try to escape from or numb yourself out to Old Brain's ultimate fear—your potential death because you aren't loved.*

SO MUCH OF OUR EMOTIONAL OVERWHELM STEMS FROM WHAT FEELING GENERATES AND WHAT REASON FAILS TO EXAMINE.

This is why you do what you do, even though you know what you know.

*The reference to death here stems from the risk to our safety as infants if no one cares enough for us to meet our basic needs of food, clothing and shelter.

Reason (New Brain) is not always right either because you are still seeing through your belief filters. But Feeling (Old Brain), left to her own devices, unexamined, will lead you astray into emotional fear bombs that never let you truly rest. And so many rocks in your pack have origins in this unexamined thinking.

The almighty challenge here is that Feeling (Old Brain) wasn't created for the world we now live in. For almost the entirety of the history of our species, our ancestors lived in 'small nomadic bands' that survived by gathering plants and hunting animals. [2] It was during that long era (almost all of the '200-page history of our species'; see page 36) that evolution shaped Old Brain. Having been forged by that environment, Old Brain works pretty well in it. [2]

Yet we now live in a world transformed by technology. I'm not saying there aren't immense benefits and extraordinary experiences to be had as a result. It is just that our biology, our biochemistry, our nervous system and aspects of our psychology have not yet evolved to always respond appropriately within such a world. It took '200 pages' to shape Old Brain (Feeling) into all she is and that final paragraph—the last two centuries—that's comparatively nowhere near long enough yet for Feeling and Reason to find a new way to function. And stress, which is another word for fear, is the result—unless we come to know our two thought systems, unless we come to know HOW we think.

THE ALMIGHTY CHALLENGE HERE IS THAT OLD BRAIN WASN'T CREATED FOR THE WORLD WE NOW LIVE IN.

Old Brain (Feeling) is a prehistoric refugee who doesn't understand the world she now finds herself in. She is overwhelmed and confused by it all. And fear and FOMO are peddled in this world which Feeling has no option but to interpret as real threats. And because New Brain (Reason) is slow to respond, many of our fears and stresses are never examined for what they really are. We cannot yet tease apart the adrenaline we make from a cup of coffee or that which we make when we are worrying about all of the tasks we still need to pull off today. We can't tell the difference between that adrenaline and the adrenaline we make when a balloon pops or that which we make when we have to suddenly swerve away from another car that has merged too soon into our lane. It's all the same to Old Brain (Feeling) and she does her best to ensure you stay alive. But this has dire physical and mental health consequences, because the relentless production of adrenaline means that your body, ever so rarely, gets the message that you're safe.

At this point in evolution, this is where we are at. Our two thought systems don't communicate with each other. Perhaps the next stage of our evolution will be best served by gradually altering us into beings where the two systems can see, understand and appreciate each other, which is somewhat analogous to the current needs of our planet. And natural selection may eventually weed out our existing separate thought system structure, as it has become somewhat maladaptive in this caffeine-infused, technologically transformed world. But remember, Old Brain evolved over the majority of the 200-page book of our species' heritage and we've only written the first paragraph of the next chapter—the beginning of our modern world. So, for now, we are stuck with these two thought systems and the gifts and challenges they bring.

With the systems as they are, we need to do our best to take responsibility for our thoughts and catch ourselves in the act, in the act of living from unexamined responses. That's the best we can do at the moment—catch ourselves in the act. Or, at least to begin with, catch ourselves as soon after the act as possible. Almost all (or perhaps even all) of what we perceive as stress comes from what Feeling (Old Brain) generates and Reason (New Brain) fails to examine. You won't stop Old Brain at this evolutionary juncture from coming up with her explanation. But you can bring Reason (New Brain) in to examine what this prehistoric refugee has come up with. And it is the time that elapses between the two—Feeling's response and Reason's analysis—where all the destruction, the overwhelm, the lousy choices and the weight of your invisible load are really felt. And the less time you spend between what Feeling generates and what Reason evaluates, the more peaceful and healthier you will be, and the lighter the load you will carry.

ONE MORE THING

Don't confuse Feeling and/or Reason (the two thoughts systems) with the voice of your Soul.

Feeling: the old thought system that has allowed our species to survive. It is a gut response, an intuition if you like, an instantaneous response. It is unconscious. You cannot direct this response. But don't confuse this style of intuition with what I refer to as your Soul.

And for those of you who have a belief system that allows for the following to exist:

Soul: uniquely you, knows the Truth with a capital T. Your essence. The eternal part of you. She is the part of you that trusts the unfolding. She has no need to stress. She fears nothing. She knows it's all FOR you. Get to know her voice.

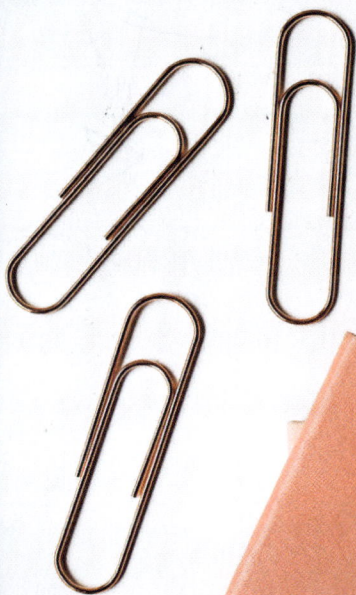

Victim mentality and people pleasing

When you're stuck in a stress cycle

One of the reasons the emotional pillar is such a key part of my work is because it is through the shifts and insights that emerge from examining our emotional landscape that we are able to make and sustain the changes we desire, deep down. And truly lighten our load. As we've discussed, our beliefs drive our behaviours. However, more often than not we have not been taught to consider what we believe about the world and about ourselves. This can make it something that's incredibly challenging to address. Some go there effortlessly, excited by what they will learn. Others are very confronted and resist. And it is important to respect and allow for whatever arises. The section 'How do you think?' (on page 205) is designed to help you better understand how you think and what you believe.

Over the years, I have come to understand that there are specific emotional patterns that hold people back from vital shifts necessary for them to get well. They are patterns that keep us locked into a relentless state of overwhelm, with all of the ripple effects you now understand this drives. There are two common ones. The first I call the 'poor me', which is someone who lives with a victim mentality (please note that being a victim of a crime or within a situation is completely different to having a victim mentality). The second is the person who relentlessly seeks approval, the 'people pleaser'.

I offer you the following with immense compassion in my heart, as these attitudes almost always stem from pain in a person's past. If you see yourself in what I'm describing, remember you do this in an attempt to ease your pain and to avoid future pain (you usually won't be able to see this though due to Old Brain having made some meanings that are not yet visible to you), and that you're not alone. We all do this. So please read this with tenderness in your own heart, the tenderness you'd show a child in pain.

POOR ME

We cannot resolve what we face—overwhelm, dysfunction or disease—when we have a victim mentality. Clues that you commonly display a response pattern based in victim mentality include a 'poor me' attitude and a tendency to feel like others owe you something. You usually refuse to take responsibility for your actions, pity yourself and want others to do the same. You share your tales of woe in an attempt to have others feel sorry for you, yet you might also believe that others are against you. When your friends or family give you ideas about ways to resolve your concerns, you take no notice and no action because part of you needs the drama. You want to create your own overwhelm in an attempt to gain attention and to manipulate others to do what you feel you need them to do, which is essentially to love you. You won't see it this way initially, though. Possibly even just reading this feels immensely uncomfortable. None of us want to see or admit to the ways in which we (intentionally or unintentionally) manipulate the world around us to get what we (think) we want. Yet when we dive into it and face it, we give ourselves the greatest gift—the gift of possibility, of unconditional love towards ourselves and those around us and the opportunity to powerfully lighten our load. There is no question that you will have had pain (see the article on page 197) but remember suffering—and so therefore victim mentality—is optional. Do you think some of your invisible load could have a basis in this type of thinking?

Having worked with patients for 20 years, those with the 'poor me' attitudes are the slowest to shift, gain insight and get well. They are so used to blaming—others and circumstances—that they struggle to take responsibility for themselves. Having worked in health retreats with people from all walks of life, on occasion I would witness someone—a grown adult—literally throw a tantrum when they couldn't get a spa treatment they wanted on the day that they arrived. In doing this, they would show me their victim mentality and their need to feel important and valued in an instant, behind which is all of their emotional pain. No adult who likes themselves

WHAT WE CAN'T SEE IS THAT WE WILL DO FAR MORE TO AVOID PAIN THAN WE WILL EVER DO TO HAVE PLEASURE.

behaves that way and there is usually an enormous amount of background stress for something so seemingly small to be the proverbial straw. So how do we end up behaving like this? Because of our beliefs and because we spend our lives in pursuit of pleasure, when what we can't see is that we will do far more to avoid pain than we will ever do to have pleasure.

I recall a conversation and an interaction with a woman who'd had a tantrum about not getting the treatment on the day she wanted. It started out with her sullenly saying 'why does this always happen to me?'—a statement based in victim mentality. This lady later apologised for her behaviour, embarrassed by what she'd said and done. I gently suggested she explore why her response was so intensely emotional as, rather than being embarrassed, it would be far more useful to her if she didn't waste this experience. And when she examined what had played out with CURIOSITY and placed her judgement and embarrassment of herself aside, what she saw was that it was a fear of being alone. She thought that if she couldn't get the spa treatment she wanted, she would have nothing to do and this stressed her out intensely—even though she knew it was what she needed. She realised during these hours of self-enquiry (it is seriously such fun to truly get to know yourself) when she sat with a pen and paper, that as a child she was regularly asked to go away from where the rest of the family was spending time. If they were at home in the kitchen and lounge room, she'd regularly be sent outside. If they were on a holiday, her parents would hang a sign in the window of their caravan, 'friend wanted', so that someone else would come along and take her away to play for the day. Imagine how that would feel to a child. So, when she couldn't get her treatment, the potential of having to be alone sparked far more in this woman than just an ordinary frustration.

And therein lies part of this message. See if you can NOTICE when you experience a response within yourself or that you display outwardly that you come to see is out of proportion from what the situation necessitated. This lady came to see how utterly painful these experiences of being ostracised were for her as a child, but that they have also fostered a warmth in her she thinks she wouldn't otherwise have. She said she bends over backwards to help out a 'few people worse off' than her, and she could see through this exploration that the common thread they all had was that they are on their own in the world. So, she'd been there for them, 'the odd bunch' as she fondly referred to them.

Again, here's an example of how from our pain contribution arises. You just want to examine the belief that will have formed from being on the receiving end of your unique experience of the kind of childhood treatment described above, because otherwise it will likely run your life, contribute to your invisible load and lead to some potentially lousy behaviours. In the case of this lady, a belief was that she was not worthy of being loved, the opposite of the truth, but which you can understand her believing, once you know this tiny part of her upbringing that she shared. It also demonstrates the immense rewards on offer to you when you go within; when you bring curiosity and a tenderness to yourself and enquire.

This woman could have just sat fuming, or really rolling out the response of someone with a victim mentality had she not done this exercise that day. She said she usually never moved past blaming others for what was happening, she'd rarely taken this type of responsibility for herself and what was happening. Not getting her treatment that day (she later found out her PA never sent the email requesting the treatment) worked out to be the best thing ever, she told me, as the real reason she must have come to the retreat was to see how her pain had created a side of herself she didn't like, one she blamed for her single relationship status, despite really wanting a partner. But now also she could see the good it had brought her—and others. You can't just acknowledge the lousy stuff that comes from awful experiences and keep blaming others (in this case, her parents) because you can be guaranteed that these almighty challenging experiences will have also shaped you in ways and developed traits in you that wouldn't otherwise be there, that you LIKE about yourself. You need to 'blame' (thank) them for these too!

Our desire to be loved, appreciated, liked, or to fit in, however you want to phrase it, and all the different ways we want to experience what is essentially love, is very persistent. You just don't want to seek it in ways that ultimately hurt you. Which doesn't just occur in what typically plays out in the lives in people with a victim mentality, but also for the pleasers.

THE PEOPLE PLEASERS

Most women were raised to be 'good girls', to do as they are told and to put the needs of others ahead of their own. And we are taught this with the best of intentions so that we grow up to be kind and functioning members of society. But what if these lessons from childhood don't just set themselves up as guideposts for your personality, but rather they become a set-in-stone way of being, way of living, that now drives your hurried, overwhelmed lifestyle?

There is an enormous difference between being a kind and selfless member of the community and feeling like your life depends on it. It is when you have zero flexibility in the way you need others to see you that the people pleaser traits take over to your detriment. Left to their own devices for long enough, these traits lead you into myriad challenges with your health from the relentless stress response this drives. On page 178 where we talked about the words we have written across our foreheads, the pleasers almost always have kind, thoughtful, selfless, giving, helpful and/or other traits of this ilk as their forehead words. You will have incorporated these traits into your identity and, sure, they are part of that. But you will also have moments where, even if it is only in thoughts that no one else is privy to, you are unkind, thoughtless and selfish. You just do your best to keep these hidden, even from yourself, because they are parts of you that you are yet to love—they are parts of you that you've made wrong because you perceive that someone who raised you would have withdrawn their love had you openly displayed this. So, you shut it down in an attempt to secure their love and now you have no other way of operating in the world for fear you let someone down, which unbeknown to you, triggers your ultimate fear: loss of love leading to death. That's why you'll do ANYTHING to avoid it. Not consciously, remember, because of the Old Brain–New Brain set-up.

> THERE IS AN ENORMOUS DIFFERENCE BETWEEN BEING A KIND AND SELFLESS MEMBER OF THE COMMUNITY AND FEELING LIKE YOUR LIFE DEPENDS ON IT.

People pleasers seek approval and will do anything, including sacrifice their own health, to avoid being seen as selfish. They have enormous trouble saying no, behind which is a fear that they will let others down, or be looked upon unfavourably. They were probably rewarded as a child for helping. The silent driver of much of their behaviour is so that no one ever 'rejects' them. This causes them to run themselves ragged trying to be all things to all people, feeling like they are never a good enough wife, mother, friend, daughter or colleague. Their invisible load is immense not only due to their beliefs about how they have to appear to others (kind, for example), but because of all of the tasks they take on to uphold this appearance.

Until you do the inner work and truly KNOW in your heart that you are enough the way that you are, that you are loved for who you are not for what you do, until you find and deconstruct the beliefs you have about who you have to be to be loved (remember the questions: whose love did I crave the most? Who did I have to be for that person? Who could I never be? See page 214), you will likely continue this exhausting and ultimately harmful way of living. Be all of those beautiful and generous traits, of course. Just have flexibility with yourself, allowing yourself the freedom to not have to display them at all times.

As Elizabeth Gilbert so impactfully says: *'The women I love and admire for their strength and grace did not get that way because shit worked out. They got that way because shit went wrong and they handled it. They handled it a thousand different ways on a thousand different days, but they handled it. Those women are my superheroes.'* [1] I wholeheartedly agree.

'Boredom, anger, sadness, or fear are not "yours," not personal. They are conditions of the human mind. They come and go. Nothing that comes and goes is you.'

−ECKHART TOLLE [2]

Reframing your stress

How heavy is your backpack?

Stress comes in many shapes and forms. It stems from such a broad range of challenges, some of which are unfortunately unavoidable. Yet, other 'stressful' scenarios are the result of our perceptions—or of our fear of being seen in a way that we can't bear to be seen in. In other words, being perceived in a way that forges a wedge between our identity and the way others view us. And if our identity is threatened, we worry that we may experience a loss of love.

Humans will do **anything** to remain true to their identity, although we probably won't be aware that this is what we are doing—at least not in the moment. This includes sacrificing our own health in order to keep everyone happy or working ourselves into a frenzy and not seeing any alternative to the way we are living our life.

A friend of mine who I admire very much has a very full life that includes full-time work, family, extended family and community service. She feels and cares deeply about many topics yet regularly laughs off what I see stresses others to the point of despair. And I often think how much we can all learn from her caring yet playful and grateful attitude to life.

I saw her recently and asked how her morning had been. She replied that it was not what she had been expecting but that it was pretty funny. She is a mother of three boys and school had been back for just over a week. When she was dropping her youngest, Master 7, to school, she couldn't get a carpark so she said to him that she'd just have to drop him off where they were and he'd have to walk just a little way to the entrance to the school. He replied, 'I'm not ready for that, Mum.' Precious soul—that comment made me smile so much.

So Mum drives around for 15 minutes and finally gets a park and can walk her youngest treasure in. She then walks back to the car and starts driving to work. She's almost at work—in a business that is run on appointments, so far from ideal if you are late—when she receives a phone call from school from her middle son, Master 9, saying,

'Mum I've split my pants.' School hasn't started yet and she's not yet at work so she drives home and fetches his spare pair of pants and then drives back to school to drop said pants off. Then heads to work again. She is now late. And it's only just after 9 a.m. She could have chosen to stress out about all of this. Or her biochemistry could have—without any conscious thought—driven her there. But it is as if her brain, at warp speed, assesses that what's unfolding is entirely out of her control and she just accepts it all as what it is and tends to it.

Is this her nature? Or a conscious decision? Is she able to do this because she doesn't drink coffee so she's not wired on adrenaline when all of these unpredicted occurrences unfold, something that sets us all up to overreact? Is it because she has an inherent gratitude that she is alive and so she just smiles—genuinely smiles—and attends to what needs attending to? All scenarios to ponder.

As far as her job goes, running late for her first client will make her late for the rest of the day. So, when I enquired about how she handled that, she said she just rang her colleague who explained to her first client what had happened and apologised on her behalf. In that small act I could see that none of this stresses her because she does not worry about what her colleagues or clients think of her. Not in a nonchalant or a disrespectful way. But because she ultimately likes herself and is comfortable with who she is. In my work with clients over the past two decades, as I explained on page 173, I've seen worrying about what others think of us almost undo some people's health. This one small example highlights how immensely our perception influences our biochemistry in everyday moments and how it is possible to perceive each situation differently.

So, with that in mind, let's explore some simple steps we can all take to help us decipher what's really stressing us out and how we can choose to take a different path so that we lighten our load both physically and emotionally. Instead of thinking repeatedly 'I feel stressed' or some variation of this, recognise how you feel.

If it is true that stress is quite often another word for fear, consider 'is this showing me something I'm frightened of?'

Q Am I ultimately worried about what someone will think of me?

For example, I'm running late and that stresses me out but when I dig a little deeper, I'm actually worried about what my colleagues will think of me. Or another example: I'm stressed because I feel like I'll let my friend down if I don't go to her birthday. When I reflect further, though, I'm actually worried she'll feel like I don't love her (easily fixed in other ways), but beyond that I can now see that I'm worried that she will think I'm a terrible and selfish person. *Determine what is really behind the stress.*

Q Is it possible that you now see you are stressed because you care deeply about the outcome or the people in your life?

Reflect on that for a moment—why would caring be stressful? The only possible reason is because you want people to see you in a certain way. You live as if your life depends on you being seen in a certain way. Perhaps as kind, thoughtful, respectful, efficient, competent, caring. Never selfish, thoughtless, self-centred, inefficient, uncaring, unkind. Imagine for a moment that the people you most love (or whose approval you most seek) in the world thought of you as selfish, inconsiderate, flaky or unreliable—how does it make you feel to imagine them perceiving you that way? This can be a great way to identify what threatens your identity and drives you to act in ways that protects what you want to be seen as. *Identify how you want to be seen by others and how you will never allow yourself to be seen.*

Now that you've determined what is really driving the stress and the ways in which you go to great lengths to protect your identity, let's explore what you can do to alleviate your perceived stress in any given moment.

Q Is there something you could do or say to communicate how much you care?

Or is a better decision for you in this kind of situation to simply let go of your concern about how they see you? For example, your job might rely on you being competent so you might feel better (perceive less or no stress) if you speak up about how much you care about your role, that you value efficiency and communicate that your lateness (or whatever else it might be that has led to your perception of a stressful experience) is not a reflection of a lack of care. Or if it is with a family member who loves you dearly for the wonderful person you are (even though you might forget or not believe this at times … or perhaps their behaviour and words don't show how they really feel, but if someone interviewed their heart, you know deep in yours that their heart would say you are wonderful), but you constantly feel the need to prove to them that you are kind and thoughtful (or some other traits) as a way of earning their love… Can you let this go and be happy knowing that you know you are a good human? That another's perception of you is based on how they see themselves and the world, based on their life experiences, not on who you actually are?

Another option as a way of relieving stress might look like this... When you fight with what is, you create stress for yourself. A whole slice of inner peace pie (nourishing pie) fills you up when you accept what you cannot change. This does not mean tolerating things that are occurring in the world that are unacceptable to you. If something wells up inside you that is intolerable to you, your Soul is showing you something you care about. It is willing you to do something to change a situation, no matter how big or how small the contribution or change.

A friend of mine is a busy CEO running a large company. So, when I saw him standing in the main street of the city where he lives, holding a bucket collecting money for a cancer charity, I was quite surprised as I would have thought he was time poor given his responsibilities with work and his family. Yet there he was. When I asked him how he'd come to do this, he said he does it once a month as it is his small way of trying to give back to a charity that is researching a type of cancer that had affected one of his family members. It was intolerable to him that every case of that disease was not yet curable, so this was how he contributed to finding a cure.

The mother of a friend of mine lost her mother at a young age. She has gone on to raise a loving family of her own, yet she has always carried a sadness with her about losing her mum and can't bear the thought of people not feeling loved. So even though she works 30 hours a week in a retail job, on the weekend she goes to a nursing home and gives a few elderly ladies a manicure because she cares

Another option as a way of relieving stress is to consider the beginning of the Serenity Prayer[1] which is:

Grant me the serenity
to accept the things I cannot change,
the courage to change the things I can,
and the wisdom to know the difference.

Diagrammatically this concept might look like this...

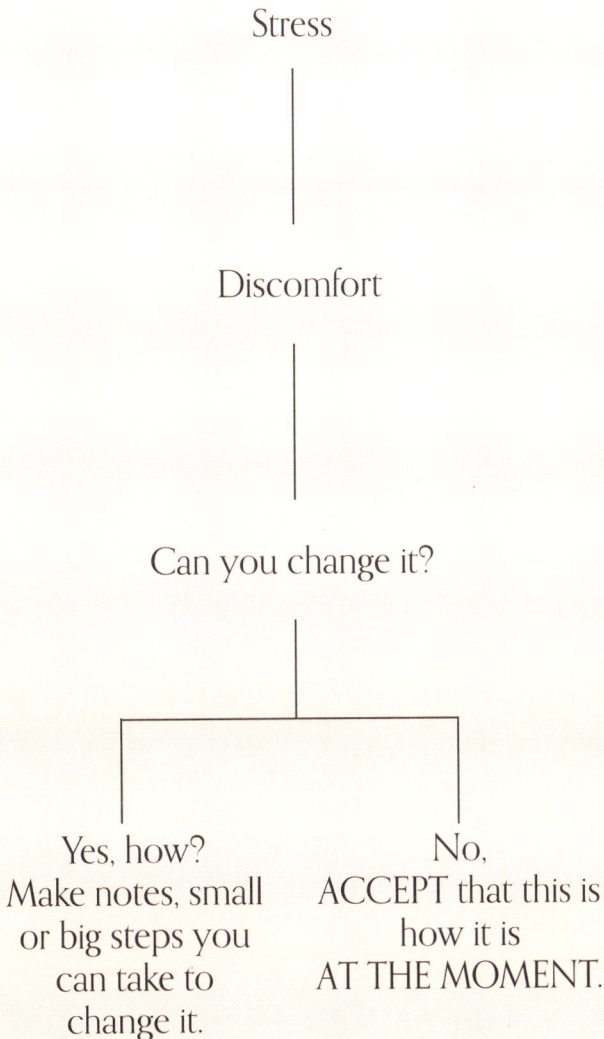

Stress

|

Discomfort

|

Can you change it?

Yes, how?
Make notes, small
or big steps you
can take to
change it.

No,
ACCEPT that this is
how it is
AT THE MOMENT.

about people feeling loved and appreciated. What was once a stress turned into a sadness and, from that, a caring 'service' has been born. Our voids create our values.

Acceptance also does not mean tolerating being on the end of lousy behaviour. No. You remove yourself from threatening environments, whether the threats or actions are physical, verbal or emotional.

As an example of how acceptance can be a way of alleviating stress: let's say you have an ageing parent and they are suffering. You choose to care for them rather than put them in respite care. As a result, you drive over 90 minutes a day to be with them and take care of their needs on top of all of your own and your immediate family's. So, you recognise that this is a source of stress for you (remembering that not everyone will find this way of living stressful). You do always have the option to not visit and care for the ageing parent. So, examine that. Is that what I want? If yes, act to change it and have them cared for by someone else. If the answer is no, accept that this is how it is right now and do your best to focus on or find the magnificent gifts within your situation. There will be plenty. For you and the parent. What a beautiful gift to give back to the person who brought you into this world or what a wonderful opportunity to spend precious moments with them that you may not get to do for much longer. You can't change that they are elderly and that they require care at this stage in their life. You can only change whether you attend to them or not and/or you can change how you see and experience this situation. It does not mean that your life is not full or very busy. But there is an enormous difference between this and being relentlessly stressed by the choices you make. Only you know what is right for you and your life—and only you can act to make changes or work on accepting what is for now, and it's in this acceptance or change that your load becomes so much lighter.

Are there some situations in your life that you need to change?

Are there some situations in your life that you need to accept for now?

Priorities and values

If your heart was in charge

In moments of overwhelm when we are really feeling the weight of the load, we might recite to ourselves that there just aren't enough hours in the day to do all we need to do, let alone want to do. But the number of hours in a day is something we cannot alter. So, a new mental approach to time can sometimes assist with a reduction in the stress we experience in our relationship to it.

Consider this: when you say you don't have time for something, what you are actually saying is that it is just not a priority for me right now. In other words, when you look at what you do each day, you will see what you prioritise based on what you make time for. Try using this new phrasing when you find yourself starting to say that you don't have time for something. And check in with yourself to see if you are comfortable with this. For example, if you say cooking is not a priority for me at the moment, are you comfortable with this? Keeping in mind that nothing on this planet can replace a nourishing way of eating and if we're not preparing our own food (or eating home-cooked meals) they are generally less nourishing, if not also filled with potentially problematic or artificial substances. If you are supporting a sick friend or relative and spending every waking moment ensuring they are cared for, you would accept and understand that cooking is not a priority for you at this time. But if there's just general life going on and you don't prioritise cooking, are you satisfied with that? You might decide, having seen it this way, that you could cook three out of seven nights. That's far better than none. Or you might see that you could cook in bulk on a Sunday and have four or five meals all set to go for the week ahead—or some version of it that works with your schedule. Consider what else you lump into the 'I don't have time' box and if you are content with what's in there.

I was speaking at an event a few years ago where I said what I asked you to consider above: 'When you say you don't have time for something, what you are actually saying is that it is just not a priority for me right now. If I look at what you do each day, I will see what you prioritise. We make time for what we prioritise.' I went on to explain that sometimes when we want to change a health behaviour, it can more helpful in fostering change to reconsider our priorities. Which always leads me to ask: what do you value? It's usually quite a productive reframing of what you put your focus on and time on. It typically improves life quality and decreases stress when we do more of what we really care about. It's usually good for our body, mind and soul.

However, I recall a lady who spoke to me afterwards at an event where I'd said this, and she was affronted at my suggestion that we make time for what we prioritise. She asked where I thought she could 'fit more in' when her days, every day, are back to back. As an aside, it interested me that she was looking for ways to fit more in, rather than cull some activities. With haste, she rattled off an example of one of her days which ended with 'and then I have to water the garden on top of all of that so are you suggesting that I just let the garden die?' I could see she was overwhelmed with responsibilities and was trying to be a wonderful person to everyone she loved, while also working full-time. She was stressed and had reacted to what I'd said because she cares so much and she'd felt like there must be more she needed to do, which felt impossible to her. It was also not what I was suggesting.

So, I asked her permission to unpack some of what she was describing with a view to lightening her load even a little, and I said she may find some of it somewhat confronting. I told her it was just my take on it and she could take it or leave it, knowing that she was just trying to do her best in life and care for those she loves. She was keen, as she was exhausted and sick of living each day in such a hurry.

I suggested that we don't tend to easily see the role WE play in all of this easily. We blame everything external to us, including what others need from us. Yet on some level, we've created— we've chosen—this jam-packed life. And there are many ways to view this type of life so let's put a few of those

ON SOME LEVEL, WE'VE CHOSEN THIS JAM-PACKED LIFE.

on the table with the view to fostering a change in circumstances or a change in perception—if changing any of this is what you want (which this lady told me she did). So even though seeing it this way can feel a little confronting, I share with you part of what she and I respectfully discussed, in response to all of the topics she brought up as blocks to her living her priorities more, rather than feeling like a 'slave' (as she put it), particularly to her family, in the hope you may also find it helpful. You'll see the essence of the Serenity Prayer in action as we want to address the things we can change and accept what we can't (or don't want to) change.

You choose to live in the house you do that requires you (and your husband) to work full-time so you can pay the mortgage. You chose to have four children, instead of none, or one or two or three and they naturally have ongoing needs from you plus expenses, being teenagers (and of course they bring you joy, as well). You choose to live in the city you do, where the cost of living is exceptionally high. You regularly ring your sister who you say 'guilts' you with every phone call, not directly saying that you don't do enough for your ageing parents, but implying such— yet you choose to ring her. You will most likely do this in an attempt to convey to her that, despite what you think she thinks of you, you are a good person, but you won't likely be aware that this is your motivation (thanks Old Brain). However, pause to consider it: why else would you ring someone you don't really want to speak to most days? You also choose your response to what she says—you choose (unknowingly) to feel guilty and to create a meaning that allows you to feel that way from what she is saying. You choose to make convenience your priority for food, rather than nutrient-density, and you can't see a way around this due to all of the other demands on your time. But just one tiny step might be that you consider ringing your sister once a week instead of every second day, which you'll be able to do if you put the guilt to bed (as a futile response to a false belief) and on the days when you don't ring her you could cook from scratch. Or you could teach your eldest teenage child how to make

a simple dinner that they are responsible for creating one night a week and your partner does another night, even just a simple BBQ and salad. And while one of them is doing dinner, if you like watering the garden you could do so a little earlier than you do now. Or if you don't particularly like it, allocate it to another of the teenagers. Your identity won't crumble if you ask for help. Yet when you are in such a rush all day every day, it can be difficult to see you have choices and ways to lighten your load through tiny steps.

A lady who was a patient of mine made what for some would be a major change, when she was pregnant with her second child. She sold what was at the time the family home and moved to a different city where the cost of housing and general living was less than where she had been living. Her husband worked full-time and she'd had to return to full-time work six weeks after giving birth to her first child, to be able to keep paying their mortgage. She was very sad about this and once she was pregnant with her second child, she took steps for her life to look differently after this pregnancy. She said she wanted at least a year at home with baby number two and then she wanted to be able to CHOOSE if she returned to full-time or part-time work, or waited longer before going back to work. And she didn't want them to suffer financially as a result of how she wanted life to be. So, after thoroughly examining their situation, she and her husband decided to buy a cheaper house, and to do that and still maintain the quality of life they wanted, they moved to a different city. This lady became clear about what mattered to her, about what her priorities were and took steps to live in accordance with what she'd identified.

She wanted the option to return to work rather than it be a need. Which brings me to another key message: when it is your preference—what you want—rather than a necessity, you feel like you have power to change your circumstances. And this entirely changes how you feel about your life as well as your day-to-day tasks.

Not everyone wants to step aside from a jam-packed life. Many will choose to stay with the rush, because they love it—they thrive in chaos—and if that is you, then that is your path, whatever that brings. There is nothing wrong with either scenario that I've described. The chaos can be a beautiful, deeply rewarding life and I know many women who live this, love it and are thriving. You only suffer when you struggle against WHAT IS, against how things are. You might have a busy, full life but it's not stressful. It all comes down to how you perceive it—if how you live is your choice or someone else's. Do you live your own values or those of another?

WHAT DO YOU VALUE?

Knowing what you value and being true to that is one of the most important paths of insight you will ever take. Living out of alignment with your values does not promote calm, clarity, or great health and energy, or lighten your load. It does the opposite. It creates a deep tension that no amount of breath-focused practices or magnesium can alleviate.

One of the most important exercises you will do as far as living a life of integrity with yourself, and therefore generating less stress, is one that helps you discover what your values are. When you explore your values, it is essential that you honestly examine your life and what it demonstrates as being truly important to you, given we make time for what we prioritise. One way to learn more about your values is to explore your answers to the following prompts: [1, 2]

Consider what you fill your space with.

Consider carefully how you spend your time.

Examine how you spend your energy and what energises you most.

Consider what you spend your money on.

Look for repetition in your responses. You may be expressing something using different language, but the value will be the same. For example, when I did this exercise, many of my answers included things like organic food, tennis, nature—for me this is all health, my version of holistic health, so I group them altogether. Group similar answers together until you have a few different categories. Then name those categories.

Examine your answers. What did you discover? Were you surprised? Or content? Is this how you want life to be? Or is there something you can now see needs to change? Perhaps you can see that some people/relationships or things are missing from your list. Maybe you'd like to spend more time and energy with your children and/or cultivating a stronger relationship with your partner or ageing parents or a new or long-term friend. There might be a hobby you love and in recognising its importance to you, you will now find a way to carve out some space for this.

Remember that a choice to do something is also a choice not to do something else. We experience much less stress when we take steps—large or small—to live more aligned with our values. What do you care about? I cannot encourage you enough to act on your answers.

Health

Career

Travel

Family

From pain we grow

The tree that never had to fight

There is a tendency today to think there is something wrong with us—inherently wrong with who we are—if we feel anything but happy, anything but coping, with anxious feelings brimming from every racing heartbeat or visibly raw, picked-at skin around our fingernails. So often, we actively avoid uncomfortable feelings and judge ourselves for feeling less than chipper in the first place. Yet from pain and from suffering comes growth. It offers us insight into what our Soul needs us to learn and forms a solid foundation for a meaningful life.

The pain might be physical or emotional. You might, for example, experience recurrent headaches. You've had tests and there's nothing sinister going on, yet they recur. Most people treat this as if they have a deficiency of painkillers rather than doing their best to get to the heart of what the headaches are really about. Is something you are eating behind them? Are your blood glucose levels unstable? Perhaps your headaches occur concurrently with your menstrual cycle. Have you been sitting at your desk for hours on end with your shoulders up around your ears? Has your day so far been filled with tasks you perceive bring pressure and need to be dealt with urgently? Has your breathing changed as a result to be short, sharp and shallow, rather than long, slow and diaphragmatic?

When we take a pill, we can miss the real message. And neglecting that, not examining that, may lead to bigger health challenges down the track, which will also add more rocks to your pack. Your body doesn't want you to suffer. It wants you to survive and ultimately thrive. It gives you pain as a way of communicating information to you that you aren't otherwise hearing. And all of it is for your growth and learning. For what happens when we overcome something? When we truly solve it? Do you typically stay quiet and clam up? No. Most people find some way to share their victory and the insights they garnered, and this fosters the assistance and growth of others.

A ripple effect occurs.

Or sometimes the pain is emotional. And it might feel like it will never end. Or perhaps it ebbs and flows, and you feel it deeply on occasions and can touch it gently on others. And yet, within it, there's a part of you that you are still to love. Sometimes emotional pain tries to guide us to see this and accept something about ourselves that we'd been judging harshly or not acknowledging up until now. Or it offers us visibility of something we are frightened of that masks itself as stress. Love is, after all, what we were born with. Fear is what we learn. And part of our journey here is an unlearning, a relinquishing of fear and the return to love. And rather than wait until our death beds, let's see the truth sooner, rather than living our whole life through the lens of our fearful, made-up stories about who we are.

Perhaps there are times when you want to run away from it all and start again where no one knows who you are. Or there's a despair that arises when you sense the incongruency between your choices and your aspirations.

All I'm suggesting is that through hardship we grow. It's not the only way, but it's a powerful one. Yet our culture has medicalised what is essentially human despair. Or we try to side-step what we're feeling with distraction. Yet despair is designed to grow and expand us, reminding us of our courage and resilience. Dealing with despair has shifted from turning to organised religion, to psychotherapy to pharmaceuticals over the past 100 years. And while each of these support systems can play a significant role and literally save lives, they each have their pros and cons (except therapy which I can only see as immensely helpful). Plus, until we (often with support) understand how we think and what's really at the heart of the pain, I'm not sure the suffering will truly subside.

Whether it is actual medication we use or other substances, or we simply fill our time so completely that we don't have the space to notice how we're truly feeling, we've created a world where people are not well equipped to deal with their emotions.

LOVE IS, AFTER ALL, WHAT WE WERE BORN WITH. FEAR IS WHAT WE LEARN.

Or even to recognise how they actually feel.

We are fortunate to live in a time where we have the option of what is, at times, life-saving medication. Yet you can choose to see it as a bridge to your healing, a call to do inner work that leads you to a deeper understanding of yourself and the parts of you that you are yet to love. And if you honestly reflect on previous pains you have gone through, and you could go back and press the 'undo' button, would you choose to take them away? Or did they alter the course of your life or teach you things about yourself in a way you never thought possible, as much as they may have hurt at the time?

When your stress or overwhelm stems from pain, always know there is someone or a support group you can reach out to. You are never alone. And talking or journaling or even opening to the pain and having a conversation with it, as odd as that may sound, might afford you a revelation of sorts from which you learn and grow at minimum, or that leads you to chart an entirely new course.

For example, I know countless people who, after a debilitating, chronic illness that they initially felt was insurmountable, embraced, often hesitantly at first, the 'feel, deal, heal' process. They did the nutritional and other lifestyle work, and went on to become health professionals as a result of what, in the beginning, was an enormous stress—life-threatening for some of them. Or there are people who suffer a horrendous injury and create a charity to raise funds to support research into a cure for that injury. They transformed some of the pain into actions that benefit others.

I'm not saying any of this is easy. It usually isn't. Yet it can be worth doing our best to consider if we are living with the belief that what occurs TO us, or rather it happens FOR us—in order for us to be the most evolved expression of our soul as possible.

This poem 'Good Timber' by Douglas Malloch [1] written in the early 1900s, encapsulates the essence of how stress can make us stronger. Its sentiments can help us to appreciate our resilience, courage and inner fortitude, and remind us to call on these traits when we need them.

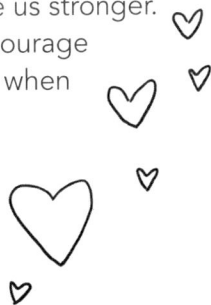

Good timber

The tree that never had to fight
For sun and sky and air and light,
But stood out in the open plain
And always got its share of rain,
Never became a forest king
But lived and died a scrubby thing.

The man who never had to toil
To gain and farm his patch of soil,
Who never had to win his share
Of sun and sky and light and air,
Never became a manly man
But lived and died as he began.

Good timber does not grow with ease,
The stronger wind, the stronger trees,
The further sky, the greater length,
The more the storm, the more the strength.
By sun and cold, by rain and snow,
In trees and men good timbers grow.

Where thickest lies the forest growth
We find the patriarchs of both.
And they hold counsel with the stars
Whose broken branches show the scars
Of many winds and much of strife.
This is the common law of life.

DOUGLAS MALLOCH

Earth overwhelm

Thinking beyond ourselves to the world around us

Humans are not the only ones overwhelmed with life and carrying a visible as well as an invisible load. If the Earth could talk, which some might suggest She can and is, I'm pretty sure She's devastated at our treatment of Her—overwhelmed by all She has to cope with, repair and maintain. And there is no question She is showing us where our attention is required for Her to stay alive. Her aliveness allows us to live. Why would we risk that? When did we move away from caring about our habitat through how we live? No species that I'm aware of destroys its own habitat. Except humans.

Many years ago, it was common for members of indigenous communities around the world, as well villages in Europe, to perform 'nature rituals' in their settlements and towns. These rituals ensured that the people who performed them, and those who participated in them, were emotionally and spiritually connected to all aspects of nature: to the land, the sky, the trees, the oceans, the rivers and the mountains. Humans lived in partnership with the Earth and their respect for Her limited resources ran deep.

In more recent times, our thinking has shifted to see ourselves as separate from and somewhat superior to Earth. Marianne Williamson [1] said this so eloquently with these words *'A new dispensation was introduced into humanity's thinking: the idea that we were not in divine partnership with the earth, but rather that the earth was given to us to be used for our purposes... That change in thinking—the spiritual rift between humanity and nature—was the beginning of our environmental crisis. Today, centuries later, that rift has reached grotesque proportions.'* There's no blame here—just identification of an initial shift in our relationship with the Earth that has now been taken to extreme lengths, primarily as a result of greed.

Never is this more obvious than when it comes to the Earth's soil, where the quality, its nutrient density for plants and hence humans, has been decimated. And if a nutrient isn't in the soil, it cannot be in our food. Lousy quality soil grows weak plants, so more pesticides, herbicides and insecticides are used to try to help the plants survive. As time goes by, we continue to learn from groups like the World Health Organisation that some of these substances are now deemed as 'carcinogenic' or 'probably carcinogenic' and many disrupt our endocrine (hormonal) system. It is devastating that they are now in the food chain.

Add to this the desecration of what was once untouched wilderness, providing habitats for fauna, housing trees and ground cover to hold carbon in the soil (where it predominantly belongs) and produce oxygen for the atmosphere. And furthermore fostering the extinction of species that would never have occurred had our perception of nature remained as one based on wholeness rather than separation—'us' versus 'them'—somehow creating an atmosphere of superiority rather than cohesion and support.

With such a loss of harmony, the Earth is overwhelmed and this must stop or we risk not just destroying more species but also killing ourselves. What is at the heart of our thinking when we, as a species, are actively destroying our own habitat? No species survives that. My guess is that future generations, with their high body toxin burdens, will look back on this time in history and wonder what on earth we were thinking. And the answer will be that we weren't.

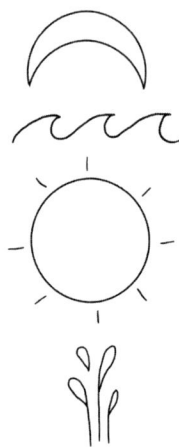

Research suggests that by-products of plastics, pesticides and some medications are contributing to the significant and continuing decrease of sperm counts. [2,3] And it's not just human fertility being affected. The estrogen-mimicking nature of some of these problematic substances in aquatic environments has meant that some fish born male develop ovarian tissue in their testes and the female fish stop producing eggs. [4] Through what we've created environmentally we are interfering with our own ability to reproduce and the data suggests that it will become harder and harder for people (and fish and many other species) to conceive naturally. Plus, every woman can choose whether or not to have a child/children. It has never been a decision to be taken lightly. The next generation needs to know that it is wiser than ever to at least pause and consider if that is what they truly want, despite cultural conditioning or familial encouragement.

So where to from here? I had the great fortune to attend Singularity University in the USA where they teach and foster exponential, rather than linear, thinking. This approach is at the heart of Einstein's concept that the level of thinking that created a problem will not be the same level that solves it. Technology that we cannot even yet comprehend will continue to be developed so that we can firstly clean up some of the mess and then secondly start to prevent it. Once upon a time not so long ago, you could never have imagined that bacteria could clean up the horrendous oil spill in the Gulf of Mexico but that's how we do it now. [5] The day we no longer need oil will also be a wonderful day and technology is taking us there. It won't be long before organ transplants are done with organs grown from your own tissues. There will be no need for anti-rejection drugs as there will be no risk of rejection.

> WE ALL NEED TO DO WHAT WE CAN WITH OUR OWN PERSONAL CHOICES TO CONSIDER AND TREAT MOTHER EARTH WITH THE CARE AND RESPECT SHE DESERVES.

It's exciting to think of what good there is yet to come, but in the meantime, we all need to do what we can with our own personal choices to consider and treat Mother Earth with the care and respect she deserves. Her load MUST be lightened.

Some simple steps you can consider taking to make a difference to the Earth's overwhelm include:

DON'T LITTER.

AVOID SINGLE USE PLASTIC ITEMS AND MINIMISE ALL PACKAGING.

Avoid purchasing vegetables and fruit that come wrapped in plastic as these foods come in their own beautiful packaging and only require a basket or reusable bag to pop them into.

SECOND-HAND PRODUCTS.

Buying pre-loved items helps the Earth in more ways than one. Reusing products protects the Earth's resources, saving resources that would otherwise be used in the production and transportation of brand-new products. As an additional benefit, buying or donating pre-loved items helps those in need. A partially-used item that still has use left in it doesn't need to go into landfill, when it can be of use to someone else, often purchased at a cheaper price than a new one.

CARRY A REUSABLE DRINK BOTTLE.

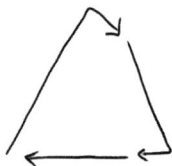

RECYCLE ANY PACKAGING YOU DO HAVE.

BUY IN BULK.

Why not try to buy in bulk? Not only does it reduce the amount of packaging you consume but it can also be a wonderfully cost-effective way to purchase products you use in larger quantities. It's better to buy one large, five kilogram tub of washing powder than to buy 10 smaller 500 gram containers, for example. Plus there are now places where you can take your own tubs and fill them up again. It saves both resources and money.

MINIMISE TAKEAWAY PACKAGING OR DINE IN.

While what you do in your home can make a significant difference, don't forget what you do when you're out and about too. Fifty per cent of all packaging is consumed by people outside the home, mostly in the form of takeaway food and drinks. It's wonderful how rapidly taking your own coffee cup if you want a takeaway coffee has become standard practice. Think like this with everything!

COMPOST OR WORM-FARM.

Recycle Nature's packaging by composting, or feeding it to the worms.

We need to care about the Earth for Her sake and our own. Without Her, we have no home. Consider how you can help lighten Her load in all of your choices.

A need for control

The antithesis of safety

It is now well established by research that we are more stressed and more frightened than previous generations, despite that same research showing we have less to be afraid of. [1] This begs the question—why? If Western life is safer than ever, why then have fear and stress escalated?

If safety really was the antithesis of stress, such improvements would have led to less stress and fear, which is the opposite of what's occurring. This suggests to me that safety is the antidote to physical stress but not emotional stress—and it is predominantly emotional stress that has its hooks into us. So, with the intention of finding yet another way to lighten the load and help alleviate stress or, better still, reduce the gushing tap to a dripping one, it might be useful to explore what potentially puts out the fire of stress for us if safety does not.

One reason I think people were less afraid of life in the past was that they had no illusion of control over it. In the twelfth century, being murdered or struck down by a crippling disease might have been more likely than it is now, but these days people don't usually write things off to Providence the way they did in the past.[2] In other words, you as an individual had no say in what occurred. It was all up to a higher power. In the past people might have had beliefs that led them to piously accept whatever occurred, no matter how wonderful or terrible it was. Or they may have lived with a fervent optimism that all would eventuate in their favour. But either way, it wasn't up to them.

Studies show that when you perceive or actually feel that you are in control of your life, stress decreases and when life feels out of your control, fear and stress increase.[3] Yet control is a perception—and completely dependent on your beliefs. You might be able to control whether you go for a walk or not today, but you can't control what might happen on that walk. You can choose which school to send your child to, but there's no guarantee that her grades will shine just because she's at that school. You can set out for work at a particular time, but you don't manage the traffic so your arrival time at your destination might be different than what you planned for. Just like the story on page 239, you cannot influence whether your son splits his pants in a before-school soccer game and requires your help to bring him his back-up pants, making you late for work.

Yet it is not just our responses to situations like these that we get to choose. There is now a level of personal choice that our ancestors would not be able to wrap their heads around. We have to (I prefer 'get to') choose the type of food we will eat and feed our children, what brand of dishwash to buy, who to vote for, and what podcast to listen to. We have much greater choice over what (or whether) we study after finishing school and the type of work we embark upon. We may even choose to go back to university to change our career in our adult years—something that was not frequently done 50 years ago. As women we can choose whether we want to have a career as well as become a mother (whether this is a source of stress for you or not, it is something previous generations were not afforded)—or whether we want to do one without the other. We can feel paralysed with the choice about whether to buy a home or keep renting, and whether having a mortgage will stop us having experiences that we value or if renting forever will mess with our sense of security.

> CONTROL IS A PERCEPTION— AND COMPLETELY DEPENDENT ON YOUR BELIEFS

To put it simply, we are encouraged to live life how we want to live it, with the catch being that we have to take responsibility for the outcome. The choices themselves might be perceived as thrilling for some and yet it's those words 'take responsibility for the outcome' that lead most to feel like they carry quite a burden. No wonder we're scared, aka stressed, and feel as if the load is forever increasing. If we make the wrong choices, if we eat the 'wrong' food or take the 'wrong' way home, and something awful happens, we have only ourselves to blame.[2] What if we choose to pursue a career first and then find it difficult to have a child later? Or study something for four years, get into the workforce only to discover we don't enjoy it? These are the kinds of choices that, for some, can feel cripplingly overwhelming and yet for others feel spacious and exciting and make life an adventure.

The deeper question here is: is part of the consideration of the role that control plays in our stress tied to choice? If so, choice necessitates decisions. And maybe we each have a different threshold for how many decisions we can make each day without it tipping us into overwhelm. Or perhaps it depends on the magnitude of those decisions and how serious or not the outcomes might be in our eyes. It seems to me that having choice is essential to our perceptions of freedom, yet, when there are endless decisions to be made in a day, day after day, year after year—some of which may significantly impact on the direction our lives take—it has the potential to add to our stress.

So, essentially, the stress from a perceived lack of control stems from fear—a fear that you are responsible for all of it and that you might get it wrong. Do you torture yourself with the anticipation of how it might go or not go? Do you fear that you could ruin it? Do you feel that maybe if you think about every possible scenario—plan for all of it in your head—you can control the outcome? If so, this attachment to control could be contributing to a significant amount of overwhelm for you. When we don't allow for flexibility—because that's what life asks of us, a degree of flexibility to roll with anything unexpected that comes our way—we set ourselves up to feel as though it's US who are responsible for the 'disastrous' outcome. As opposed to just something that happens in life that we could never really plan for in the first place and can't control.

It is possible that a perceived need for control is generated from what was said to us as children. 'You always ruin things' might lead someone to believe that they had better control everything so that they don't ruin it. 'If I could just keep everything under control, that worst outcome I'm imagining might not eventuate'. Or maybe a child lived in an environment where a parent was very controlling and so, through observed behaviour rather than actual words, they absorbed the belief that this is the way that life is supposed to be lived. The responsibility of this kind of belief system is exhausting and futile.

In how we live now, there is no question that an individual's perception of control has been shown to be important for and contributes to their capacity to have healthy (rather than harmful) emotional responses to challenging situations.[3] Plus, it appears to give us better immune function and less anxious and depressive symptoms.[4] But are we missing the point by looking at it this way and fostering a collective belief system that only sets us up for more stress? Have we almost ruined our capacity to enjoy our time on Earth by establishing, in the first place, a belief that we can control things?

Choice does not equal control. When you look at life logically, the only thing you can control—and only up to a point—is yourself. You cannot control what another human will say or do or how the weather will be. So, creating what is essentially a false belief in our ability to control outcomes related to others has set us up for a world of responsibility and stress. We are each responsible for our words, our behaviour, our efforts, our ideas, our actions and the consequences of our actions. We are not responsible for nor can we control those factors in others: their words, beliefs, ideas, actions or the consequences of their actions.

WHAT IF INSTEAD WE CULTIVATE BELIEFS THAT WE CAN HANDLE AND COPE WITH WHATEVER COMES OUR WAY?

Self-efficacy is a term used to describe a person's beliefs and perception of their ability to have an impact on events that affect their lives. It is your belief in your effectiveness and ability to manage your own life, as well as deal with individual tasks competently. In the context of stress, self-efficacy describes your beliefs about your ability to cope with stressful scenarios.[5] Which leads me to my next point…

I am very passionate about language and the way we use words as they convey so much to our own nervous system (and also others). And for some of you, this next sentence might seem like basic semantics, but hear me out. Is there a difference between your

perception of BEING IN CONTROL and your perception of your ability to HANDLE what comes your way?

These things are worlds apart for me. So my question is, would we have far less emotional stress if we were taught that we cannot control anything except for some aspects of our own body and mind? For example, you can choose what you eat but you cannot choose if that food gives you reflux or not; you can choose how you respond to the news of interest rates rising but not whether they rise or not; you can choose how you respond to the news of a loved one dying but not whether they die or not. What if instead we cultivate beliefs that we can handle and cope with whatever comes our way? Otherwise it wouldn't come our way. And what if 'emotional health strategies' became a subject at school with as much value placed on it as English?

We aren't given anything we can't handle. It is our beliefs that might lead us to feel like we can't handle something. It's the beliefs. It's always the beliefs. Perhaps this structure can stand on its own or perhaps it needs another layer of belief behind it to give it strength, one I've alluded to throughout these pages: that life does not happen TO us, but instead life happens FOR us. It's not that you have to, it's that you get to, before your turn on Earth is over.

What if we set ourselves up psychologically and with the effort we put in, to do what we can to contribute to the outcomes we want, but ultimately, we TRUST the unfolding of life? Consider all of this in the context of Nature. Life supports each and every seed to become the tree it was programmed to be. You could say that a seed becomes the best version of itself. And life supports a rose bud to open and become a rose—humans don't direct that to happen. It just happens because every rose bud has been designed to become a rose.

LIFE IS HAPPENING FOR YOU, NOT TO YOU.

So surely then it follows that the more we relinquish control and trust in our nature—the way a sapling might have to deal with cyclonic winds, drought and floods on its way to becoming a tree— our ability to handle what comes our way increases. We too are here with the capacity to become what we were designed to become and live our very best life. If we continue along this line of thinking, we may begin to trust that life is throwing things our way in order to help us become the best version of ourselves we can be—to peel back a layer that we've created around ourselves that is actually no longer necessary and based on fear. That the things that happen in our lives are taking place in order for us to bring light to the false and limiting self-beliefs that are hidden away in Old Brain and running our lives so that the reasoning abilities of New Brain can face, deal with and put to rest those made-up stories that are making us feel overwhelmed or stressed or unhappy in the first place. Our separation from nature (discussed on page 261) has not done us any service, ecologically or environmentally, and it has led us to forget that we human beings are subject to the same laws of Nature as all other parts of Her.

Ultimately, all of this fear, all of this stress, stems from a lack of trust. A lack of trust in ourselves and our own resilience and courage and strength. A lack of trust in our natural processes, for the seed that we each are, to become the tree we are meant to be. Sometimes those cyclonic winds bend us a bit out of shape across our years on Earth, but that doesn't disfigure us—it only makes us stronger, as the poem on page 258 suggests. If we allow it to.

Imagine when you are born, you are shaped like an egg and your shell is perfect. You know the truth of who you are, you know you are special yet also no more special than anyone else. You know the love that you are because anything else to your newborn egg self is not possible because you don't have a paradigm for that. But as life continues, and you try to make sense of your environment, you create beliefs about who you must be for others to be the way they are. And each of those limiting beliefs (they are limiting because they limit what you believe you are capable of and how you see yourself, others and the world) are like dents in the eggshell around you. Not divots in YOU, but in the lens through which you see the world. The dents happen to (for) all of us, no matter how calm or chaotic it is for us growing up, but they

happen to create a polarised response within us and give us the opportunity to sort them out later—learning and growing from the insights.

These beliefs about ourselves that are generated from the polarised perception either denigrate us (you become too humble or too self-minimising) or inflate us (you feel superior). You either go too low inside yourself or too high. Either way it is a movement away from equilibrium, away from the Truth. So, then life starts unfolding and things start happening and most people's brains perceive 'it's happening TO me'. It's not. It's happening FOR you, in the hope that you gain visibility of the dent in your eggshell, a response of Old Brain, created a long time ago in an attempt to protect us from a perceived lack of safety (love) which is ultimately perceived as a threat to our very life. It's all just trying to wake us up to return you to your full egg shape. And to the Truth. And the Truth is Love. Which is why I KNOW WITHOUT A DOUBT, that it's all FOR you. You can't control life. All we can do is care and do our best and learn and grow and contribute. And TRUST you can handle what comes your way. Our tiny brains cannot possibly know better than the power that exists in Nature that grows a seed into tree. That same power is in you, doing all it can to help you fully blossom.

I do believe it is the illusion of control that is at the heart of so much overwhelm and the invisible load. Most people will tell you the opposite of stress is calm; I'll suggest it is trust. To trust the unfolding of it all because when we can trust, there's no reason to stress. And if this is a struggle for you, it can help to remember that every ending is a beginning somewhere else and that there are two trillion galaxies in the universe.

THANK

YOU

Dear Reader

Thank you for having the courage and compassion
to come on this journey.

I know that some of these words may, at times, have felt confronting, or as though someone pressed on your tender spots. I hope you have discovered, however, that leaning into those moments of discomfort can bring about so much growth. When we use the pain to explore our reactions, to enquire within so we better understand the 'why' behind them, we can entirely transform our experience of everyday life—and, in turn, how our body responds.

I also hope that between these pages you felt less alone. We may feel, at times, as though we are the only ones carrying an invisible load. We don't see how many people are silently fighting to hold up the same weight, people wondering how on earth they can maintain the face—and the pace. Cultivate such kindness towards yourself and others knowing each one of us is expressing our joys, pains and the responses we've chosen thus far. Some are fighting quiet battles unknown to others and we are all simply trying to navigate the path as best we can.

This journey took us through all aspects of your invisible load starting with exploring what your personal backpack is comprised of. As you read through the articles in the Your Load section, you might have identified as being a Rememberer; a Rememberer of the bills, for the children, the work, the social calendar and the health of those you care about. And perhaps you recognised that the Rememberer role both fills you up with a sense of care and responsibility, but also that it might be depleting your health and adding to your invisible load. Hopefully you have some new insights into how to reduce the weight of being a Rememberer all of the time.

Stress has a profound effect on our health, and the thoughts we think alone can impact how we physically feel. In the Body Load section, we looked at how to spot the physical signs of stress—whether this is an increase in bloating or IBS-type symptoms, headaches, skin breakouts or PMS. We also explored in detail the role stress plays when it comes to the health of your hormones, your thyroid, your gut and your liver. When these organs and body systems aren't functioning optimally it can be almost impossible to not feel the weight of your invisible load. The physical symptoms our body gives us can be an insightful opening through which to explore our burden and a highly effective way to begin to lighten our invisible load. Never forget the power of the breath in decreasing the stress response. Simple breath practices can go a long way to alleviating some of the physical symptoms you experience, even while you look for the deeper messages your body might be trying to tell you.

We think our stress comes from everything 'out there' but the only person who gets to decide if you have a stress response, or not, is you. Through well-meaning intentions, we create beliefs about ourselves and who we have to be to feel loved and to feel safe (which as you now know is often wrapped up as one for a human). It is the relentless expression of unexamined beliefs that truly sits at the heart of so much of our stress.

In reading this book you have begun to do the inner work; to shine a light on the parts of yourself that you'd rather keep under wraps, or that you may not have realised even existed, to gain a greater insight into why you do what you do and why you feel the way you do. You have begun to bring your whole self to the table in an honest and unapologetic way. I encourage you to keep going. Notice the things in this book that hit a nerve for you and explore them further— whether this is with a psychologist, a trusted friend or by continuing to read books that speak to your heart. When you see where you may be creating meanings in response to others that feel hurtful, ask yourself what else could be going on for them, and then explore how you created that meaning in the first place. And do all of this with immense kindness towards yourself, remembering we are asking our extraordinary Old Brain to operate and keep up in a very New Brain environment and this can be confusing at times. Yet with gentle awareness we will begin to evolve our way of thinking. Live in touch with the awe in the gift of this.

And remember, you can't get it wrong, this beautiful, indescribable experience called life. See if you can apply the idea that what occurs isn't happening *to you*, but rather *for you*; for your Soul's essential evolution in Her remembering of Truth, of LOVE. Whether the aspirations you have for your life have occurred as you imagined them or not, trust that you have and are all you need right now. Because when we can trust, there is no need for stress.

With much warmth,

Dr Libby x x

Treat yourself
as the precious
person you are.

DR LIBBY

About Dr Libby

Nutritional biochemist, author and speaker

Dr Libby Weaver (PhD) is one of Australasia's leading nutritional biochemists, an author, a speaker and founder of the plant-based supplement range, Bio Blends.

Armed with an abundance of knowledge, scientific research and a true desire to help people regain their energy and vitality, Dr Libby empowers and inspires people to take charge of their health and happiness through her books, live events and nutritional support range.

Having sold over 450,000 books across New Zealand and Australia, she is a twelve-times bestselling author.

A respected international speaker, Dr Libby's expertise in nutritional biochemistry has led her to share the stage with Marianne Williamson, Sir Richard Branson and Dr Oz. She is regularly called on as an authoritative figure in the health and wellness industry and has been featured in numerous media publications including *The Times*, *The Huffington Post*, *Sydney Morning Herald*, the *Australian Women's Weekly* and she appears regularly on breakfast radio and television.

With a natural ability to break even the most complex of concepts into layperson's terms, Dr Libby's health messages embrace her unique three-pillared approach that explores the interplay between nutrition, emotions and the biochemistry of the body.

It's no surprise that when it comes to achieving and maintaining ultimate health and wellbeing, Hollywood stars Deborra-lee Furness and Hugh Jackman describe her as a 'one stop shop' in achieving and maintaining ultimate health and wellbeing.

BIO BLENDS

High quality, plant-based supplements.

For thousands of years, people having been harnessing the power of plants to help heal the body. Yet today, most supplements on the shelf are made in a lab, using synthetic ingredients. Bio Blends are different—every supplement is made entirely from plants, foods and herbs; substances the body recognises. Dr Libby scoured the world to find the highest quality ingredients and, using her twenty years of clinical research and experience, formulated the range of Bio Blends products to help you enjoy optimal health.

Calm Restore

Ease anxious feelings, naturally. Combining a potent blend of the highest quality herbs known for soothing the nervous system, Calm Restore supports the body to ease symptoms associated with anxious feelings.

Meno Magic

Natural menopausal support. Designed to work with your body. Meno Magic contains five carefully selected ingredients that work together to support the body's adaptation to hormonal changes occurring with menopause, easing the symptoms often associated with this transition.

Liver Love

Supports liver regeneration and detoxification and assists your liver to process the problematic substances that could be contributing to your headaches, gut problems, such as bloating and constipation, irritability, fatigue and congested skin, just to name a few.

Cycle Essentials

A potent blend of foods, plants and herbs which promote healthy progesterone production and help you address PMS, period pain, bloating, sugar cravings and mood fluctuations, leading to a period that simply shows up.

Organic Daily Greens & Radiant Reds

Precisely formulated to contain a powerhouse of antioxidants, substances that help to combat premature ageing. This delicious powder can be enjoyed daily in water or your favourite smoothie.

Organic Zinc

Zinc is involved in over 300 processes inside your body and most people today aren't getting enough of it. This superstar nutrient works with your body to help you have a healthy immune system, experience great energy, achieve optimal digestion and have radiant hair, skin and eyes.

Skin Nutrition

A nutrient-rich formula with a combination of healing plants that work to improve skin radiance and tone, reduce redness and increase blood circulation—think better nutrient delivery to the skin and hair follicles.

NEW • NEW • NEW • NEW • NEW • N

Calm Restore

Ease anxious feelings and support your adrenals, naturally

The thoughts we think have such an impact on our health. Whether it's anxious thoughts or a general feeling of overwhelm and stress, our body can interpret this as danger and keep us on high alert. This only amps up our feelings of anxiousness or overwhelm and can have a real impact on our health.

Combining a potent blend of the highest quality herbs known for soothing the nervous system, Calm Restore works to support the body's response to stress—taking the edge off and easing the uncomfortable symptoms often associated with this.

Calm Restore supports the body to:

- Reduce anxious feelings and irritability
- Experience relief from symptoms of short- and long-term stress
- Recover from daily physical and mental stresses
- Wake up feeling refreshed, energised and restored
- Restore healthy sleep patterns and improve sleep quality
- Promote a sense of calm by relaxing the nervous system

When we have less anxious or frazzled feelings, we're able to think with clarity, sleep more restoratively which helps promote better memory, and we're able to approach our daily stresses with greater resilience.

If you're feeling wired but tired, this is the blend for you.

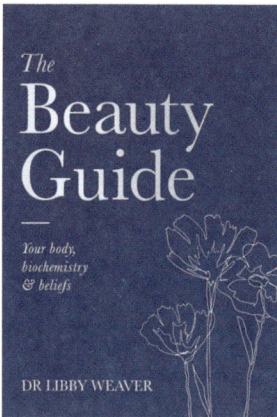

The Beauty Guide

For too many of us today, our thoughts are consumed by the things about our appearance we want to change or cover up. But what if these frustrations actually offered us a pathway to accessing our true beauty? *The Beauty Guide* offers beauty solutions and wisdom that will help to transform the way you feel about yourself.

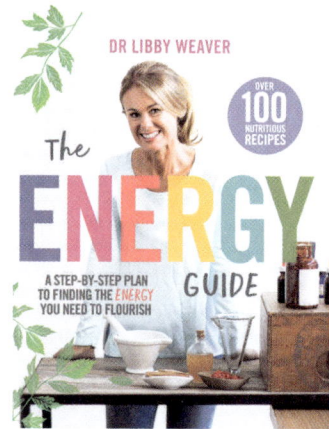

The Energy Guide

Authoritative and compassionate, *The Energy Guide*, which includes over 100 recipes and meal ideas, will help you to reboot your diet, improve your sleep, understand your hormones, reduce your stress and transform the way you think about your energy and your wellbeing.

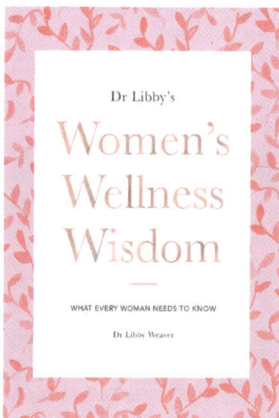

Women's Wellness Wisdom

A definitive guidebook for women, *Women's Wellness Wisdom* includes beautiful imagery, step-by-step guides, worksheets and real-life examples, helping you uncover the sources of your challenges and empowering you with the knowledge to better understand your body. Learn what women of all ages need to know from this inspiring book.

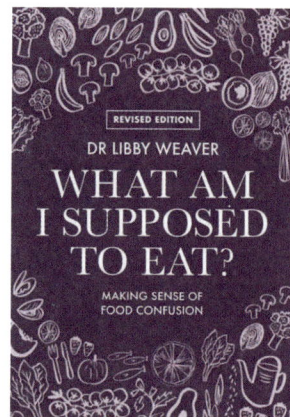

What am I Supposed to Eat?

For many people, deciding what to eat is often filled with confusion, fuelled by temptation or convenience and leaves them begging the question, *"So, what am I supposed to eat?"* This book is a fork in the road when it comes to better understanding your food, your body, your appetite, your emotions and what is best for you to eat.

ALSO BY DR LIBBY WEAVER

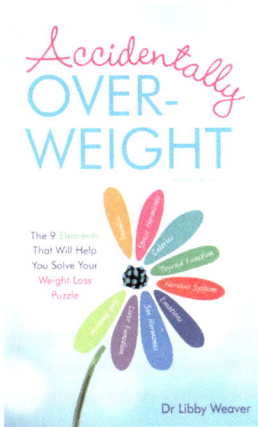

Accidentally Overweight

Accidentally Overweight explores the must-know nine factors essential to successful and sustainable weight loss. They include stress hormones, sex hormones, thyroid function and gut bacteria.

Rushing Woman's Syndrome

Rushing Woman's Syndrome offers you real solutions to both the biochemistry and the emotional patterns of the rush. What you need to do in a day may not change but how you show up can revolutionise how you experience each day and how others experience you.

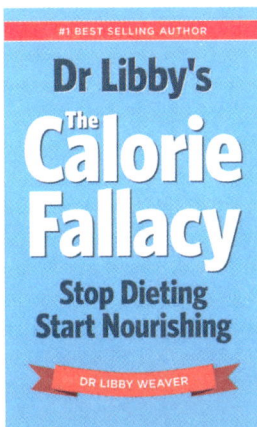

The Calorie Fallacy

This book arms you with the wisdom to stop dieting and depriving yourself and start thriving. Stop dieting and start nourishing and live with a new freedom in your relationship with food and your body.

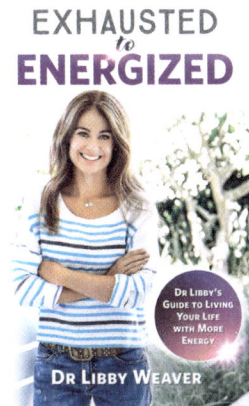

Exhausted to Energized

Everything in life is more difficult when we are exhausted. *Exhausted to Energized* offers you simple but powerful strategies to help liberate you from exhaustion and live a life with more energy.

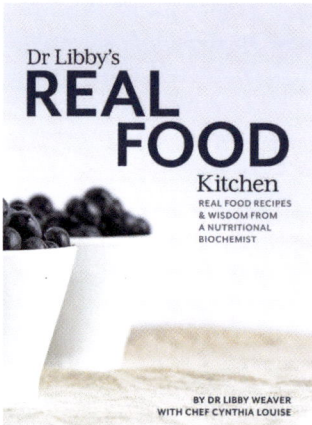

Real Food Kitchen

The *Real Food Kitchen* will inspire you to take better care of yourself with the delicious and nutritious recipes featured. Packed with nutrition information as well as recipes that are firm family favourites that have been 'real food chef-ified', you will love using this beautiful cookbook.

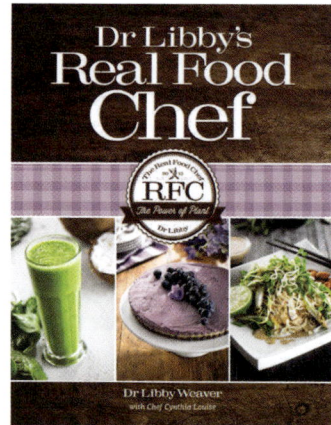

Real Food Chef

The *Real Food Chef* is a beautiful book that will revolutionise the way you are nourished. Filled with delicious and nutrient dense meals, drinks, snacks and sauces, this book educates and supports you to embrace a real food way of eating.

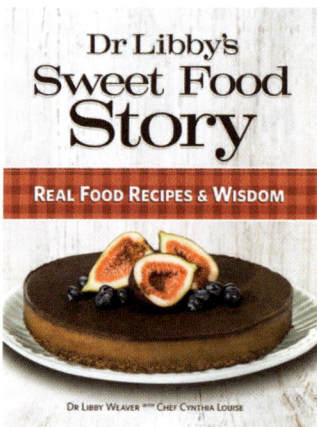

Sweet Food Story

Many people make great food choices for breakfast and lunch, and then at 3 o'clock in the afternoon they feel like someone else has taken over their body, their desire for sweet food can be so intense. The *Sweet Food Story* cookbook was created with this in mind, as a way of educating and supporting you to eat sweet food that serves your health.

References and resources

I am regularly touched by the number of people who, after reading one of my books, write to me saying that it's like I've described their life or peeked at the pages of their journal. If, after reading *The Invisible Load*, you would like to delve further into your physical or emotional health, I encourage you to check out my website where you will find all of my other book titles, weekend events, tours and courses.

If body fat or energy challenges are a daily battle for you, you might benefit from *Weight Loss for Women*, which is a nine-week practical online course overflowing with guidance and tuition to help you solve your weight loss puzzle.

Take a look at the blog too at:
www.drlibby.com

I also post health information on social media.

Connect with me there at:

www.facebook.com/DrLibbyLive
And on Instagram, find me as @drlibby

My passion is to educate and inspire, and to help people change the relationship they have with their bodies and their health and put the power of choice back in their hands. It is an honour to assist you in your optimal health journey.

I have cited some books and papers in this text and they are listed in full here if further reading in a particular area interests you.

Over the last 25 years I have read in excess of 10,000 books and research papers that have inspired and shaped my work. I have done my best to include those who have been instrumental in contributing to my work, as well as to this book.

There is additional referencing on my website: www.drlibby.com

REFERENCES AND RESOURCES

Dictionary definition of Load and Overwhelm:

https://www.merriam-webster.com

Are you the Rememberer?

1.   https://www.worldcat.org/title/managed-heart-commercialization-of-human-feeling/oclc/9280843

Racing to keep up

1.   Gardner, D. (2008) *Risk: the science and politics of fear.* Melbourne: Scribe Publishers.

How we end up exhausted

1.   https://www.ncbi.nlm.nih.gov/pmc/articles/PMC2248601/

The load on your liver

1.   https://www.invivoclinical.co.uk/files/nalini_chilkov_-_estrolobolome.pdf

Is it my thyroid?

1.   https://www.ncbi.nlm.nih.gov/pubmed/10403185

Gut health

1.   https://www.ncbi.nlm.nih.gov/pmc/articles/PMC5772764/

Leaks and gut bugs

1.   https://journals.sagepub.com/doi/10.1177/1362361399003001006

2.   https://www.ncbi.nlm.nih.gov/pubmed/23201091

3.   https://journals.plos.org/plosone/article?id=10.1371/journal.pone.0171206

IBS

1.   https://www.healthdirect.gov.au/irritable-bowel-syndrome-ibs

2.   https://www.ncbi.nlm.nih.gov/pmc/articles/PMC3921083/

3.   https://www.ncbi.nlm.nih.gov/pmc/articles/PMC4303825/

4.   https://journals.plos.org/plosone/article?id=10.1371/journal.pone.0186629

5.   https://www.ncbi.nlm.nih.gov/pmc/articles/PMC4438173/

6.   https://www.ncbi.nlm.nih.gov/pubmed/27397586

When did sadness become stress?

1.   http://allmylooseends.com/2014/03/lights-wink/?fbclid=IwAR1ZZq7fyPFL92Ac OOyl-xCvfO7k_RQ1N3lLikS7pij-zYpuTRcskYP2xKY

REFERENCES AND RESOURCES

Pain versus suffering

1. Frankl, V. (1984) *Man's Search for Meaning*. New York: Simon & Schuster.

2. Niebuhr, R. *The Serenity Prayer.*

3. https://www.psychologytoday.com/au/blog/some-assembly-required/201401/pain-is-inevitable-suffering-is-optional

How do you think?

1. https://emilymcdowell.com

2. Gardner, D. (2008) *Risk: the science and politics of fear*. Melbourne: Scribe Publishers.

Victim mentality and people pleasing

1. https://www.elizabethgilbert.com/wisdom-age-women-dear-ones-the-other-day-someone-asked-me-why-i-had-ded/

2. Tolle, E (2003) *Stillness Speaks*. London: Hodder & Stoughton.

Reframing your stress

1. Niebuhr, R. *The Serenity Prayer.*

Priorities and values

1. Demartini, J. (2013) *The Values Factor*. New York City: Penguin.

2. https://drdemartini.com/value_determination

From pain we grow

1. Malloch, D. 'Good Timber'. First published in the *Detroit News*.

Earth Overwhelm

1. Marianne Williamson lectures

2. https://academic.oup.com/DocumentLibrary/humupd/PR/dmx022_final.pdf

3. https://www.gq.com/story/sperm-count-zero

4. https://uwaterloo.ca/news/news/wastewater-treatment-upgrades-result-major-reduction

5. https://www.scientificamerican.com/article/how-microbes-clean-up-oil-spills/

A need for control

1. Gardner, D. (2008) *Risk: the science and politics of fear*. Melbourne: Scribe Publishers.

REFERENCES AND RESOURCES

2.   https://www.theguardian.com/books/2008/mar/09/society

3.   https://www.ncbi.nlm.nih.gov/pmc/articles/PMC2944661/

4.   https://www.apa.org/pubs/journals/features/int-int0000035.pdf

5.   https://www.mentalhelp.net/articles/self-efficacy-and-the-perception-of-control-in-stress-reduction/

General References and authors who have influenced my thinking:

Frankl, V. (1984) *Man's Search for Meaning.* New York: Simon & Schuster.

Gardner, D. (2008) *Risk: the science and politics of fear.* Melbourne: Scribe Publishers.

Robbins, A. (1992). *Awaken the Giant Within.* London: Simon & Schuster.

Roth, G. (2009) *Women, Food and God.* New York: Scribner.

Williamson, M. (2011) *A Return to Love.* New York: Harper Collins Publishers.

Live speakers who have influenced my work:

Dr John Demartini, Empyreance program.

Tony Robbins

Marianne Williamson

TED Talks

Acknowledgements

My Old Brain, New Brain, Heart and Soul are deeply thankful to those who helped bring this book to life: Sarah, Maddy, Bree, Chris, Steph, Sabine and Karloski. Thank you for all of the big picture and little detail work you did on the pages or behind the scenes. And thank you for your encouragement and care.
I appreciate you all immensely.

♡

notes

_____

_____

_____

_____

_____

_____

_____

_____

_____

_____

_____

_____

_____

_____

_____

_____

_____

_____

notes